YOUTUBE MARKETING STRATEGIES

BY: NICHOLAS HARVEY

CONTENTS

INTRODUCTION

With a proven YouTube marketing strategy, you can increase traffic to your website — Youtube is one of the most popular internet video sharing websites in the world. Marketing through YouTube is certainly the best way to provide customers information about your business online.

Effective video marketing helps to showcase your products. Marketing on video sharing websites has become one of, if not the most effective, online business promotion technique in the world today. Because of the presence of tough competition business, it is practically impossible to run one successfully without proper marketing techniques. An innovate strategy on how to market through YouTube can skyrocket revenues and profits. No matter what kind of business you are running, YouTube marketing strategies can help you reach a large population.

A strategy for marketing through YouTube can increase the online visibility of your product, allowing nearly any business to easily create new customers. Newspapers and magazine advertising campaign publication takes days to accomplish. Now, similar information can be shared instantly on the internet through videos. Online video marketing is wide reaching, uncomplicated, and effective.

Websites like YouTube have been used worldwide to share and enjoy video content. Be it a funny video of your child or a video tutorial, YouTube has everything that is needed for efficient video promotion. This website is very useful for promoting videos and creating a well bonded relationship between the video up loader and his or her viewers. Members of YouTube interact through comments and email. YouTube increases business's website presence and enhances its image for prospective clients.

If you have a business and are looking for effective

ways to create a marketing campaign, learn

YouTube marketing strategies first. Video marketing is becoming more and more popular because of its low initial cost and minimal maintenance.

However, YouTube marketing has become an essential part of any successful network or online marketing strategy. YouTube, according to Alexa analytics data is the number three most visited website in the world, ranking after Facebook and Google.

We all know that YouTube is also owned by Google, the most important search engine in the world.

Alexa reports that each visitor spends an average of 24.02 minutes per day searching or just browsing YouTube. Many network marketers have experienced significant breakthrough in their business using video marketing on YouTube or on any other video sharing site.

Why YouTube?

Videos ranks higher on Google search than even the most SEO optimized and back-linked blog post or article. Even the SEO guru himself - Rob Fore and many of the industry's top leaders use videos on YouTube to communicate with their lists and subscribers.

Network Marketing success depends largely on building relationships, when potential prospects see your face and hear you on a YouTube video, that builds instant rapport and a bond with your audience. They feel they know you and it takes your believable factor to a whole new level, higher than just words on a blog or post. People need to see and relate to a real person.

Any lead found via YouTube marketing is also a more superior and qualified lead, and automated rapport builds with daily visitors to your channel which can actually happen on auto-pilot for years, after posting the video.

On this powerful and under-utilized channel of

YouTube video marketing, a video post takes less time to actually produce or create than an article. An average well crafted article or post, takes about

two hours or more, while high-ranking videos takes an average of three to five minutes, especially if it's for generating leads or traffic to another portal like your blog or other websites.

Usefulness Of Youtube

Videos, long or short, can have a positive impact on your website's traffic or for conversion. Apart from reading content, consumers also love watching videos. This is easier to do, and hence gaining popularity, compared to reading a text-based advertisement.

If you are not yet into video promotion or not aware of it, then it is time to focus on this emerging platform and adapt video marketing to your digital marketing trends.

You can add loads of information in a simple and short 3-minute video which would present things in an entertaining and engaging manner. Customers always love being entertained, and what better way to inform and educate than videos? However, when making videos you should have a clear picture of the product/service you are offering.

Many clients are keen to know the benefits involved with your product/service before they are ready to spend any amount and that too online.

The benefits of online video advertising:

• High percentages of audience are known to interact with videos, browse through the ads, click the video control buttons and more.

• CTR (Click Through Rates) are always higher for videos than the text, banner, and image ads.

• Viewers watch the video ads. Video ads pave two thirds of the way.

• Specific demographic and the consumer based category can be targeted through video ads.

• Provides great benefit to advertisers as executions can be easily slotted online, saving time and money otherwise spent on creating a whole new execution.

Posting a video on YouTube takes on a life of its own as this video can then be viewed by thousands of YouTube users which in turn would be shared on numerous websites, blogs, and email in the world of Internet. You need to tailor it according to the user's needs and requirements, which would send the right message to the YouTube crowd. This simple move would then start generating traffic from the people who visit YouTube daily.

Anyone who is watching your video is a potential customer, and this is why you shouldn't forget to include your website address or contact information in the video.

- Using YouTube for Brand Awareness

Many advertisers often use YouTube for advertising their brands to create awareness. Here it's not about individual videos or services; rather it's a chain effort to promote the brand in the same way that is seen on television.

The idea is to not focus on any single video, rather you should always try to think bigger and make

a visionary path for your brand. Single videos might get lost in the heaps of videos but the brand videos don't.

Brand Awareness Videos are more about entertaining which is a simple approach where the brand makes an image for its viewers to enjoy.

- Using YouTube for Advertising Products

If you fall under the category that pushes individual products, even then YouTube should be the best place for you as this requires direct approach that makes videos informative plus educational while focusing on brand and entertaining.

- Using YouTube for Retail Promotion

Many brands use YouTube to promote retail

stores. In this case, the videos produced can be in general or specifically targeted or for short-term promotions.

To put things clearly, it's a form of direct advertisement which wouldn't really attract viewers. However, approaching it differently by showcasing the claims of 10-20% off or weekend specials would do better.

- Using YouTube for Sales

Using YouTube for generating sales for products/services is a terrific idea and can be implemented at the grassroots level itself. All you need to do is show the product in action or provide a clip of the service related to the question and generate sales by directing the viewer to your website.

The best idea is to showcase the product video, how to use, upgrading and other such stuff. Create a shorter version of the videos which you can promote by using YouTube Ads, but focus on the goals of the product in the video which the user wants to see and it'll gain more YouTube viewership.

- Using YouTube for Product/Customer Support

Many companies show themselves as extending support, which is not true; only some companies extend their support for existing & upcoming customers. In this case, YouTube helps generate new focus for businesses in support sectors.

Focus on the customer problems, Q&A, and try to produce the videos addressing these issues and methods. If you can do so, then it will not only help your customers, but it will help you in future. Always make sure that you provide useful service related videos that will reduce the company's costs.

All is Possible with YouTube Videos!

TIP: Now you can embed YouTube Support videos in your Website where customers can view them in the support section. What matters here is that the customers should get their problem solved by viewing the Video. No expense incurred here as the customer solves 70 - 80% of the problem by viewing the video itself.

- Using YouTube for Training Purpose

Now, you can use YouTube videos for internal and external purposes like product training

for meetings, conferences, etc. Doing so will save you a lot of time.

Recently digital marketing companies like MOZ, Distilled, and Blue Glass use these methods to reach consumers for conferences and much more! Apart from these, people who are unable to attend conferences due to various reasons can purchase these informative videos online from the relevant stores.

Using these informative videos in YouTube is gaining popularity, as now the videos are available for rental purpose where the user can watch them as and when required.

Apart from these you can also use the YouTube for

communication with employees and even for the purpose of recruitment.

TIP: Instead of holding a big meeting and addressing all concerned, companies can record the address and post it on private channels on YouTube where employees can watch

them when required comfortably from their own desk

A Mindset Shift is Needed to Breakthrough in YouTube Marketing

We need to break free from the barriers and fear of video marketing. That fear of criticism, ridicule and mean comments, our physical appearances, lack of confidence and the thinking that our videos have to be perfectly scripted and well produced. Be genuine, real and relatable. People distrust guru-like personalities. Be yourself and do it afraid.

Keys to Success in Implementing a YouTube Video Marketing Strategy:

- Use Keyword Research to find what people are

looking for and to optimize your video in the title, description,script, and actual video title for the chosen keyword.

- Always direct your prospects to your capture page and put the link in the first part of the description.

- Use Social back-linking like TribePro to increase back-links to your video URL and increase ranking on both YouTube and Google.

- Time stamp your video with your keyword in the description and YouTube actually adds extra back-links. (More details in Traffic Mojo Series in MLSP)

- In creating the video, be yourself, be excited, speak with confidence and do it afraid, till you get comfortable!

- Build commonality, mention your location, smile, and greet your audience.

- Your video must have a purpose, so introduce it, provide content and give the call to action.

You have to direct them to the purpose of your YouTube marketing video.

The Best Kinds of YouTube Marketing Videos

Sometimes we get stuck thinking, "what should I make a video on?"You can make a video on anything, but for business purposes, some great topics are:

• Marketing Strategies, Marketing Mind-sets and Aha Moments

• Company, Books, Product and Leader reviews

• Value-based training or Personal developments videos.

• Pieces of training or webinars provide hot, fresh and relevant content or ideas.

If you are new to this, keep it simple - listen to a webinar or wake-up call and make a one minute video about what you learnt on that call or training, upload it, post it to your Facebook wall, ask a couple to marketer friends to check out. Do this three to five times in a row to breakthrough and become comfortable on video.

Experience a breakthrough in your network or online marketing business, create a video post for your channel and start your YouTube Marketing today. More and more business owners are slowly discovering how YouTube marketing is going to benefit their business.

How Does This Apply to Internet Marketing?

Video online is rapidly growing and seems to be getting bigger and bigger. It is time you were creating your own YouTube marketing strategy in order to promote your business or products. Think about how you can best use video in your business.

You can use YouTube advertising to spread your message and drive traffic back to your website. Have you thought of all the sales you could be getting with your YouTube marketing videos?

What about all the subscribers that could come

your way from YouTube traffic. The more subscribers can mean more profit for your business. You need to start using online video today.

Internet marketing YouTube traffic will result when you create some videos of your product or service. Video marketing is not expensive and YouTube hosting is free. This is not the case with some other sites however and they could burn a pretty hole

in your wallet. Not want you want at all when trying to keep costs down in these tricky economic times.

Are you starting to see why getting involved with YouTube marketing will actually be beneficial to your business?

Generally it is easier to rank a video than say a website or blog. The more people that look at your video on YouTube, the more visitors you will get back to your website. As more people view your video it will move further up the rankings also.

You will need some special YouTube marketing software to create your video content. Obviously you will need some kind of video camera. Yes, you can use your smartphone or even one of the small Flip type cameras. However, for better quality a camcorder is always my preference.

If your video becomes popular then you can earn some revenue from this as part of the Google/YouTube revenue program.

Text sales pages into video content

Whenever I am faced with a long sales page, I tend to scroll to the end of it pretty quickly. There is just too much to read and most of it is just not interesting enough. It would be much better to use one of the best kept YouTube marketing secrets and that is to convert the text sales page into a video sales page.

Moving content engages better with the viewer. Nobody likes to read so much text, but if you have a voice in the background or even a demonstration of the product you are promoting, then you are giving out a great visual experience.

People are naturally visual people, having grown up with the cinema and television. We love to watch video content so do not be afraid to create videos.

Video testimonials

Have you ever received feedback in written form for any of your services? If so then go and dig these out because you can turn them into video testimonials. You show the text on screen and speak out loud

the testimonial. This could be added of course to your video sales page.

Video articles

Do you publish articles or any kind of written content? Again this is a great candidate for YouTube marketing video content. Turn those dry text articles into video articles and get them loaded up onto YouTube.

Presentations

Ever given a presentation to an audience? Well now is the time to take the video camera out and film your next one. You can load this footage onto YouTube of course as part of your YouTube advertising strategy, but why not package it up into a product also. You can sell this on your website or on a DVD.

Lastly, you need to imagine how a YouTube marketing video strategy is going to benefit your business. Do you really want your competitors to get ahead?

Try turning those dry text based sales pages or articles into online video content and watch your profits climb.

CHAPTER 1

WHAT IS YOUTUBE MARKETING

YouTube marketing is a digital strategy that takes advantage of your audience's proclivity for video, allowing businesses to promote their content and grow their brand.

Simply put, YouTube marketing is a way to get your business noticed, and show people what you've got!

Let's talk about YouTube. We know it, we love it, we've probably all watched one too many funny cat videos on it. YouTube is an excellent source of entertainment, but it is also an increasingly important tool for business owners and internet marketers.

In fact, almost half of all marketers (48 percent) will be adding YouTube to their marketing strategies this year, according to the State of Inbound Report.

With YouTube marketing, you can increase brand

awareness, improve your SEO (search engine optimization), and present your content in a way that is compelling, unique, and shareable for viewers. Still not convinced?

Why invest in YouTube marketing

You might be thinking, "That all sounds great, but my consumers probably aren't on YouTube."

Guess again! YouTube has an enormous and very diverse audience consisting of over one billion active users. Collectively, those users watch one billion hours of video every single day, generating billions of views. That's a massive amount of content reaching viewers!

Video marketing is huge right now. Recent statistics show that video content is an effective form of marketing — and the demand for it is growing rapidly. Did you know that one-third of all online activity is spent watching video? Or that 53 percent of consumers want to see videos over other content types?

Your audience's preference for video is undeniable. And with YouTube marketing, we can not only create the type of content your customers want but use it to get your business ahead of the competition.

But there is a little bit more to YouTube marketing than just uploading your videos and seeing what happens.

If you want to use YouTube and video marketing to grow your business, you're going to have to learn how to:

1. Optimize your YouTube channel

2. Produce optimized video content

3. Utilize good YouTube marketing techniques

Let's grow your business with YouTube marketing!

Youtube has massive traffic and viewers, with over 1,325,000,000 people using Youtube. There are currently 300 hours of video uploaded to YouTube every minute of every day – 5 hours of video content every second! Which only validates the fact that video marketing is a growing trend – the numbers say it all.

Video is where the web is going. The move toward video has reached critical mass, a tipping point where the momentum will swing and things will all start to speed up.

For online and offline Business owners and internet marketers, YouTube Marketing is an essential strategy to take advantage of the web's massive shift toward video. That's why it's so important to learn and test some strategies and to get help from Digital Organics right now. It will give you a huge leg up on your competition, helping your business to move forward.

Think about it: As others struggle to establish their presence on YouTube, you could have an established position with a top-ranked video. Believe us, it's hard to knock a popular YouTube video out of the number one spot, but our Online Marketing techniques can get your listed and ranked in Google and bring your website more visitors. You'll benefit from a rise in your Bing or Google ranking. And it goes without saying that a page one Google rank is as good as gold.

Did you know that the top listing in Google's organic search results gets an average of 34% of the clicks? The second gets around 20%. The third gets 13%. That means all the rest of the results on page one (paid and organic) fight over the remaining 16%. The paid results only get about 5% of the traffic — it's a horrible affliction referred to as "ad blindness."

The Best Marketing Practices on Youtube

- ### Channels vs. Pages

It's important that you reset the way you look at YouTube channels versus YouTube pages as you begin to think about YouTube strategically. You need to think of YouTube as a kind of second website. Your channel is the homepage that anchors your YouTube website. Your videos are the webpages.

Every video you have on your channel strengthens the website, because every video points back to your channel page. The more authoritative your channel/homepage becomes, the easier it becomes for your site to rank.

Here's a key thing to remember, the rules of good web design apply in YouTube the same way they apply elsewhere.

To build authority, you need to keep your videos relevant to the theme of your channel. Whether your niche is model trains or growing azaleas, you should create a specific channel for each major topic.

In other words: There's no benefit to throwing a ton of unrelated videos on one channel. That would simply dilute your channel's authority.

- **Video Creation**

This is usually the first big challenge that comes up when a first-timer wants to launch a YouTube Channel.

Most people are a bit camera-shy and don't feel comfortable having their face plastered all over YouTube. Well, here's the good news – you don't have to become a YouTube celebrity. In fact, it might actually be better if you don't appear in your YouTube videos.

But before you even begin the creation process, you have a very important decision to make: What purpose should your video serve?

Here's a list of goals you might want your video to achieve:

• To build your website's readership – Your video is a great opportunity to encourage viewers to check out your "real" website. This move can often lead to an opt-in or even a sale down the road.

• To capture a lead – You can also ask for an opt-in directly in the video. Simply draw attention to a link listed below your video, and explain what visitors will get once they've opted in.

In addition, it's really important that you track all of the leads you get from YouTube – because they're educated about your product. And an informed lead is worth roughly 10 times the value of an uneducated lead.

• To build your website's brand – While most brands do this almost exclusive, it's really hard to tell if you're accomplishing anything because it's not measurable in any way.

• To make a direct sale – There's absolutely no reason you shouldn't present a CALL-TO-ACTION in your video and provide a link that goes directly to an order form. We're actually shocked to see how few people actually do this!

To sell an affiliate product – Here are the three best affiliate marketing strategies used on YouTube:

1. Open box buy – In these videos, affiliates will simply open a product in a YouTube video, showing viewers exactly what's inside the packaging. Then, they'll provide their affiliate link to that product on Amazon or elsewhere.

2. Reviews – YouTube reviews are another great way to relieve buying anxiety and provide an affiliate link.

3. Training videos – Lastly, many affiliates make money by simply training viewers how to use a complicated product, and then sending those educated leads to their affiliate link.

- **Video Sequence**

Timing is everything, and sequencing is the key to making sure your timing is perfect. While we're on the subject of timing, the ideal length of your YouTube video is right around 3 minutes.

If yours is an in-depth training video, you may have to go considerably longer. Still, we recommend that you keep it under 10 minutes if at all possible.

Here's a 7-step sequence you can use in your video marketing strategy:

1.   Intro and branding – In the first step of this sequence, you'll want to inform viewers about who you are and where else they can connect with your brand – e.g. Facebook or Twitter.

2.   Tell them what's in it for them – Immediately after your brief intro, you need to explain 2 things: WHY they should watch AND how long the video is going to run (most people don't like open-ended commitments).

3.   Give them the value – The third step is where you actually deliver whatever information you promised in your title. YouTube videos are great places to explain concepts.

So if your video is titled, "What Is Facebook Timeline?" this is the part where you'd explain all the key ins and outs of Facebook's latest overhaul.

4.   Recap with a conclusion – Referring back to

our old marketing proverb, this is the part where you, tell them what you told them. You may say something like, "Today we learned what Facebook Timeline is and how it works."

5. Advise them – Offer some advice based on the information you just gave the viewer. It may be a recommendation, encouragement, or even a warning; you just need to impart some form of helpful advice.

6. Call to Action (CTA) – You didn't produce this video just because you had some extra time to kill, did you? Of course not. That's why you need to memorize this mantra: READ, LEAD, or BUY.

ALL of your videos should have a CTA that asks viewers to become a reader, subscribe to your list, or buy something. It's amazing to see how many YouTube marketers miss out on this step completely!

7. Drag at the end – Once you've delivered the CTA, leave a little dead time for emphasis, maybe a minute or two. It may just be silence with an arrow pointing down to the link you're promoting.

You don't want the video to simply end because Google will immediate suggest other videos inside the player – and your link will disappear.

YouTube is the New Twitter

And finally, this is one very important YouTube concept you need to know: YouTube is no longer just a video search site – it has aspirations to become a top-tier social networking site as well.

That means, the more friends, likes, viewers, and engagement your videos get, the better they will rank.

If you're looking to maximize your YouTube channel's social engagement, internet video marketers have given positive feedback about Tube Toolbox. This service is notable for being highly effective and for playing by the rules of

YouTube's terms of service.

Why Have Your Own YouTube Channel?

So, here's the thing, you don't want to start an online business without considering the use of videos. You may haven't noticed it but everywhere you look, this form of content really draws in a lot of people as compared to the sole use of articles and images. Adding videos to your website is a game-changer and you can search for the numbers if you're in doubt.

Now, the question is, where and when did this video marketing revolution began?

You guessed it right; the biggest influential factor that launched this form of marketing was YouTube. Of course, there were other websites that offer video upload and streaming features but they weren't as strong as YouTube.

Considered as one of the biggest social media platforms, YouTube really changed the image of internet along with its contemporaries like Google, Facebook and Twitter – the titans of the modern World Wide Web. For the past decade, the internet has been transformed from a source of information into haven for different ventures like entertainment, music, games and business.

As mentioned earlier, videos attract people and people means potential client, potential client means opportunities for conversion and conversion means more profit. That's how simple it is.

But how important is it to have your own YouTube channel?

Here are some tidbits you might want to know:

What makes a website stand out?

- **More content**

It's the content and videos. Especially coming from YouTube, it actually speaks more than a million words and that's what you want for a solid content. Adding a YouTube channel to your website to fill your quality videos in will make people go back as often as they can to get information.

- **More traffic**

Logically speaking, as more people go back to your website for the videos or even to your YouTube channel, traffic will also increase. People might look for the videos on YouTube at first but as they find your videos useful, they will eventually follow the link to your website and that can drive more traffic. The secret is patience.

- **More connections**

This is where having your own YouTube channel gets more interesting. The connectivity factor in YouTube makes it a reliable social media platform. Unlike random posts and tweets, videos can easily relate to the viewers. They get to be familiar with what the videos are intended for and at times these viewers get hooked by it. That's the reason why it's necessary to make clear, high quality videos. Videos that don't just promote or entertain but videos that really connects to its viewers.

- **More revenue opportunities**

If you know how to manage your YouTube channels, you can actually earn more revenues. You see; videos that are being watched more often can be used as an advertising tool and YouTube actually pays the subscribers that get a lot of hits on their videos. How to get money from YouTube might fall on a different topic but at this point, we just want to stress out the importance of creating high quality and interesting videos.

YouTube isn't just a video sharing website, it's already a form of media and it has already changed the lives of the people who used this as leverage for success. With a little hard work and dedication – you can reach it too!

THE IMPORTANCE OF YOUTUBE IN MARKETING

Video has become an integral part of Internet users' online experience, and no site hosts more videos than YouTube. The site boasts more than 3 billion video views per day, making it an excellent place for marketers to find consumers. Its reach is global, too; 70 percent of its traffic originates outside of the United States, making it more

than a place to find only American customers.

Viral

YouTube is the home of the viral video, the term for a video that spreads quickly to a large audience on the Internet. Marketers can use other social media avenues, such as Facebook or Twitter, to direct consumers to YouTube videos as a way of trying to get the videos to catch fire with the public. Especially popular videos make it to the YouTube home page, further strengthening traffic.

Channels

On YouTube, you can host your own channel. This allows you to centralize an online location for all manner of videos related to the product or service that you are marketing. You can create a series of related videos this way. It also helps you keep a fresh library of videos. You can update, revise or create completely new videos about your product or service, while maintaining an outlet for the older, related videos. Marketers have the option to establish a free user channel, such as the one many individuals create, or to pay, a fee to host a branded channel, which gives marketers more options and features to improve their pages.

Measurement

One of YouTube's greatest strengths is the way that it allows anyone to track how many views each video is receiving. There are no complicated searches or evaluations necessary. Instead, the number of viewers for each video is posted right beneath the video image. This allows marketers to gauge instantly how widely their videos are being received, and how successfully they are finding an audience. You can also see how many people are recommending your video or commenting on it.

Miscellaneous

In addition to brand channels, YouTube offers other options for marketers attempting to reach the site's many users.

These opportunities include buying advertising on the home page or buying advertising that runs beside certain videos. Marketers can also use keywords so that, when certain search terms are used on YouTube, it will trigger their videos to appear as an option for users.

Marketers then pay based on how many users choose

to watch their video.

BENEFIT OF YOUTUBE MARKETING

The iconic red play button has been a cultural staple for over a decade. Artists, comedians, and celebrities alike, including Justin Bieber and Shawn Mendes, have launched their careers through YouTube.

From a business perspective, it's hard to deny the effectiveness of video marketing. Businesses of all sizes can adopt a video marketing strategy as part of their inbound marketing strategy and enjoy these amazing data-backed benefits of using YouTube:

1. Capture Attention

No matter who your audience is, they are likely using YouTube. In fact, according to Alexa, YouTube is the second most visited site. Your potential for exposure is extraordinary.

However, you're facing a lot of competition. Statista's July 2015 research found that a whopping 400-plus hours of video were uploaded to YouTube every minute. In other words, coloring inside the lines might get your content lost in the shuffle.

Instead, focus on creating captivating videos that stand out from what your competitors are doing. Research their strategy, then identify opportunities they're overlooking or subject matter you can cover in a more in-depth, engaging manner.

2. Generate High Traffic Volumes

According to YouTube's research, there are over a billion users, and they watch a billion hours of video per day. That's a lot of traffic opportunities.

Your video marketing content has the potential to reach billions of viewers. Of course, that is highly unlikely, but the promise of generating high traffic is definitely plausible.

Not only does YouTube provide a cost-effective dissemination strategy, but its reach is far more comprehensive than regular television and cable stations.

The slow death of cable continues. In fact, Google's 2016 research found that six of 10 people prefer online video to live TV. What's more, predictions suggest that by 2025, half of people under 32 years old will not subscribe to a pay TV service.

It's no wonder why 81% of businesses use video as

a marketing tool, which is up from 63% the year prior, according to Wyzowl's State of Video Marketing 2018 survey. Video is not just a trend; it's a necessary aspect of your marketing strategy from now on.

There are several kinds of videos you can create to take your marketing strategy to the next level

such as the following:

• **Explainer video** - Show how your product or service addresses common pain points for your audience.

• **Training video** - Demonstrate how customers can use your products or services to gain the most benefits from them.

• **Webinars** - Educate your audience on a specific theme or topics they want addressed.

• **Customer stories** - These share your real customers' obstacles and highlight how they achieved desired results with your product or service.

3. Experiment with Viral Marketing

The term "viral" often conjures up this idea of a massive burst in popularity surrounding a piece of video content. From sneezing baby pandas and moms wearing Chewbacca masks to Charlie biting his brother's finger and dancing to that catchy chorus of Despacito, there's no doubt in the potential of viral content on YouTube.

For example, the aforementioned Despacito music video generated over five billion views, making it the most watched YouTube video of all time.

In a perfect world, you can churn out video content that would be seen by millions of leads ready to close deals and skyrocket earnings past your revenue goals. But viral marketing is not just about racking up millions of views.

Viral marketing is the strategy you build around how your audience can spread information about your products or services. This information can spread through word of mouth, and it is most likely to be shared with each of your audience member's social networks.

Fortunately, you can use your YouTube content in many ways that can spark shares. For example, embed your video content within relevant blog posts or share a link to a relevant video in a LinkedIn group discussion.

The main aspect to focus on with video content is delivering value to your audience. If your viewers find your content informative, insightful, and entertaining, they will share it.

Many times, people who receive a YouTube video that has been passed on from a family member or friend share the video with others, thus creating a ripple effect.

Why Things Catch On, outlines the 'STEPPS' framework for creating contagious content:

• **Social currency** - People want to look like they're in the know, so informational content will be shared widely and reach a lot of people.

• **Triggers -** Ensure your audience is triggered to

think of your brand based on certain context that aligns with your products or services.

• **Emotion** - Feelings are as powerful as function, so inject video content with real emotions.

• **Public** - Consider how to design campaigns that are inherently simple to promote and easy to spread.

• **Practical value** - Expertise-driven, educational content that delivers usable, actionable solutions is likely to be shared.

• **Stories** - Use narratives to deliver ideas because people love to communicate and share through stories.

4. Gain ROI From Multiple Video Marketing Channels

It's no secret that when you create video to market your business, you need to see ROI. Otherwise, you're wasting your resources.

The good news is that, as found by Wyzowl's State

of Video Marketing 2018 survey, 78% of marketers say video gives them a good ROI.

There are several channels you're likely investing in or thinking about investing in. This includes hosting services like Vimeo, which is the second largest video hosting platform

 and plenty of social media platforms.

Thanks to the advent of live streaming features from platforms like Periscope and Facebook Live and short form videos from Snapchat and Instagram Stories, the landscape for video content has radically changed.

This is why you should be engaging in various channels of video content, like IGTV and Facebook Live, while also maintaining a strong YouTube strategy. YouTube is your bread and butter for your video campaigns, while the other video channels should complement and support your YouTube content.

Simply put, creating and posting a YouTube video

is a powerful asset to any digital marketing strategy. The widely recognizable format makes it the perfect ground for staging a product or service.

Plus, the intuitive algorithm YouTube uses can boost your viewings by suggesting your video content to viewers who are watching related content.

At CES in 2018, YouTube Chief Product Officer Neal Mohan said that more than 70% of view time on YouTube is caused by their AI-driven recommendations.

5. Boost Search Engine Rankings

Google acquired YouTube in 2006 for $1.65 billion in stock to stay dominate in the world of search. The fact that YouTube videos are often ranked high on Google's search pages shows that building your video marketing strategy around this platform can yield real SEO results.

Plus, look at the trends of searcher behavior. Cisco's 2017 study projects that video will represent 80% of all internet traffic by 2021. The growing interest in video is likely encouraging Google to rank sites offering video content higher.

As you develop your YouTube channel, you further establish credibility in your industry and grow brand awareness. With the right tactics, you can drive a lot of traffic to your videos on your channel and, in turn, to your website.

Treat your YouTube videos like your blog content. Start by conducting keyword research, then optimize your YouTube content by using your keywords in the title, description, and tags.

Aside from maintaining your YouTube channel, you should also identify how you want to include your YouTube content within your website's content.

Here are a few awesome SEO benefits you can enjoy by adding video in your website content:

• **Build backlinks -** Providing high quality video within your website content can earn quality backlinks within your industry, which helps boost your ranking.

• **Reduce bounce rate** - Including a relevant, valuable video on your webpage will keep visitors around longer, especially if they watch the video through to the end.

• **Earn high ranks in video suggestions** - If your video is super relevant and optimized, Google might rank it under their suggested videos, which usually ranks after the featured snippet and before the top organic result.

6. Integrate with Your Social Media Marketing

Not only are YouTube videos easy to share through your social media, but video is also wildly popular in the social world. Just for Facebook alone, users view eight billion videos daily.

Social media users generally prefer sharing video content over any other content format. According to research from WordStream, social video generates 1200% more shares than text and images combined.

Likes and other forms of social media engagement outside of sharing are also valuable. Animoto's 2015 survey found that 84% of consumers say they liked a company video in their newsfeed, and nearly half of them personally share company videos to their feeds.

By distributing YouTube videos on other popular social media sites such as Facebook, Twitter, LinkedIn, and Reddit, your business exposure can instantly increase exponentially.

The more popularity your YouTube video receives, the higher it will rank. As the video increases in popularity, the better the chance that associated links will be clicked, which will also grow your online business presence.

7. Reach Global Audiences

YouTube is an international sensation, reaching countries around the globe. It is accessible anywhere, on every device. And this shift toward mobile use is boosting the platform's popularity even more.

Research from App Annie found that YouTube is the top app on Android and iOS based on peak time spent in a month, average monthly time spent, and peak monthly active users in a month.

The online video giant is available in 76 different languages and 88 countries. Because of this level of availability, the exposure potential for your video content on YouTube continually provides one of the most effective marketing tools available – on a 24/7 basis each day.

A YouTube video strategy a must have, especially if you're marketing to global audiences.

The Takeaway

As you can see, the data says it all: YouTube is your best channel to use for video marketing.

You can enjoy boosts in SEO, build your traffic and brand awareness, expand your social reach, market to audiences overseas, improve your ROI, and diversify your video marketing strategy with multiple channels.

It's time to hit the play button on your video marketing strategy.

EIGHT (8) GREAT BENEFITS OF USING YOUTUBE FOR BUSINESS

As a small business, you must continually think of ways to get your products and services in front of as many people as possible, all without breaking the bank.

Using YouTube for your business can be a cost-effective way to grow it if used regularly as part of your marketing strategy.

Online retailer ModCloth drove 4000 subscribers

and 1 million YouTube views, resulting in more sales, for just a ninth of the cost of their average search campaigns.

Not sure if YouTube can help grow your business? Here are 8 benefits that YouTube can provide to your business:

1. Tap Into The Horde of YouTube's Traffic

Online video is growing exponentially, with over 4 billion videos viewed daily. If you use YouTube for your business, you can easily reach your audience, both by creating videos, and advertising on other people's videos.

• YouTube is the 2nd largest search engine and the 3rd most visited website worldwide, behind only Google and Facebook respectively.

• 1 billion people visit YouTube each month globally

• 100 hours of video are uploaded every 60 seconds to YouTube

• According to Nielsen, YouTube reaches more US adults aged 18-34 than any cable network

Video-streaming platforms like YouTube have become so big you're guaranteed to find a group of people who will become your raving fans and customers, as long as you educate, entertain and provide solutions to their problems.

Want to get the more views for your channel? We recommend this fantastic course from Udemy. Set up a channel, increase views and much more: YouTube Masterclass – Your Complete Guide to YouTube

2. Marketing On YouTube Will Help You Get Found On Google

Due to Google Universal Search, videos, images, news, books and local searches are blended together in Google's search results, so as to provide the most useful information for people searching.

You might have noticed that videos are appearing

more often in Google's search results. This shows that Google considers video to be as important as text-only pages.

You can take advantage of this by writing high-quality articles on your site and creating complementary videos in YouTube. Doing this will build backlinks to your site, meaning you get found on Google more often by people searching.

By utilising YouTube as part of your marketing strategy for your business, you're also increasing the authority of your website. The more authoritative your website is in Google's eyes, the higher all your pages will rank in the search results.

Fun fact: Over 60% of searchers click on the first 3 results on Google, and over 90% of all Google searchers click on the first 10 organic results.

Four (4) Top Tips For Using YouTube To Increase The Authority of Your Website:

- **Get other website owners to embed your videos on their websites**

Every time someone embeds your video in their website, it counts as a vote in favour of your video. The more people who embed your video, the higher it will rank in the search results, as Google gives more authority to websites that have great content, which is updated regularly.

- **Associate your domain name with your YouTube channel**

Associating your website with your channel will tell YouTube that you are the official representation of your brand on YouTube. This results in more relevant video results pointing to your business when someone searches for your brand or terms relating to the services you offer.

- **Get your videos shared on social media platforms**

Social media metrics are a factor taken into consideration by Google when ranking pages. If you can create high-quality videos that entice others to share, you're signalling to Google that you are producing content that is valuable to your target audience.

- **Give your audience more options to consume**

Providing your audience with a variety of ways to consume information – including text, video illustrations and audio cues – will increase the overall engagement your videos receive, as you are catering to different learning styles.

Fun Fact:

• 65% of people are visual learners

• 30% of people are aural learners

• 5% of people are kinesthetic leaners

3. Your Content Never Dies

Using YouTube for business can help you to re-purpose content you've already created without the need to spend a lot of time or to invest inexpensive equipment.

Re-purposing content you have already created is

an effective form of content marketing, as you can reach an audience that will love that particular type of content.

For example, this blog post, can easily be re-purposed into many formats including:

• Podcasts

• Infographics

• Presentations

• Video series

This approach enables you to create at least 4 pieces of content from just 1 idea, resulting in an engaged audience who can easily digest the information you provide for them.

Want to get the most out of Youtube for your business? We recommend this fantastic course from Udemy. Set up a channel, increase views, and much more: YouTube Masterclass – Your Complete Guide to YouTube

4. Grow Your Audience Worldwide

This is one of the biggest benefits of using YouTube for business.

Consistently creating video content opens the door to new visitors who would never come across your business any other way. Through YouTube, you can reach a worldwide audience even if you only speak one language.

If you're a native English speaker, you're at an advantage, as it's difficult to capture the huge English-speaking markets (30% of all YouTube views)

if you can't write or produce excellent content.

In addition to this, if you include closed-captions on your videos, you can also reach new audiences as you are catering to people with different needs.

Research now shows that videos with closed-captions receive 4% more views and subscribers than those without.

Fun Fact: 80% of people who prefer to watch video with closed-captions enabled don't have hearing impairments.

It's also crucial to include several call-to-actions inside your videos, with annotations that link to:

• Other videos

• Content on your website

• Email auto-responder series

• Products and services on offer

5. Build Your Email List in YouTube

Another benefit of using YouTube for business is the ability to build your email list as you continue to provide valuable, engaging content.

Use software that allows you to embed your sign-up form directly into YouTube videos. A video can be stopped temporarily for a viewer to enter their email address and subscribe to your list, before they continue.

Using this approach makes it easier than ever to

build your email list, whilst providing engaging video content your audience will love.

6. Your Audience Will Promote You and Buy from You

Videos with a personal touch help to increase conversions. People buy from those they trust, and that trust is built by you relating to them on an emotional level.

Research now shows that for professional services and general companies if you are driving traffic to a landing page with a video of a person in the company speaking about the product or service, it can dramatically increase your list of leads and sales.

Want to get the most out of Youtube for your business? We recommend this fantastic course from Udemy. Set up a channel, increase views and much more: YouTube Masterclass – Your Complete Guide to YouTube

7. Target Your Audience with AdWords for

Video

With Google AdWords for Video, you can get laser-focused access to your audience by advertising on videos your audience are more likely to watch and search for.

The biggest advantage of AdWords for Video is that you'll only pay for engaged views.

An engaged view occurs when a viewer watches your ad for at least 30 seconds. In other words, if your video ad is skipped, you won't pay anything.

Take a look at how Rokenbok generated 50% of their customers from YouTube due to their video advertising campaign.

The biggest benefit of AdWords for Video is the potential to grow your audience through 'earned views.'

These views are free and are earned when someone who chooses to watch your video ad, then goes on to watch one or more videos on your YouTube channel within a 7-day period.

If someone watches 2-4 videos on your YouTube channel, they are far more likely to subscribe to your YouTube channel.

8. Make Money with AdSense for Video

Creating regular video content gives you the opportunity to earn some money directly from your videos, through Google's AdSense for Video programme.

Fun Facts:

• Over 1 million content creators from 30 countries around the globe are earning money simply through YouTube videos

• Thousands of channels are making six figures a year

You can use Google AdWords and AdSense for Video together to make some money back from your video campaigns too.

It works like this:

(1) Viewer sees your video ad in another video and

clicks on it.

(2) You pay for that click as part of your campaign budget.

(3) Viewer proceeds to watch your video, viewing the ads from other content creators that are enabled to display on your videos. (can be disabled)

(4) Viewer clicks or watches those ads and you are paid 68% of the ad revenue.

This means that you can run AdWords campaigns for your videos, whilst making money by allowing others to advertise on your videos.

As you can see YouTube is a viable platform for growing your audience and business in a number of ways.

If you invest the required time to learn the main components of the platform, YouTube will show itself to be a worthwhile addition to grow

ADVANTAGES & DISADVANTAGES OF

YOUTUBE MARKETING AND HOW TO LEVERAGE THEM

YouTube was founded in 2005. In its first few years, the video hosting site was perceived as a source of entertainment. Some may still think of it that way, but today, YouTube can be integral to your social media marketing.

Yet of all the social media apps, YouTube still has the stigma of focusing on cat videos and video game let's plays.

That doesn't mean you should give up on this form of social media marketing, though. You just have to be smart about it.

While video marketing can be daunting to some, the practice can pay dividends. By monetizing your videos, you can increase ROI.

Advantages of YouTube Marketing

1. Free to Use

YouTube is completely free to use. (YouTube Red,

a subscription-based music streaming service, is not.) You can make an account or link your Gmail, then upload or watch as many videos as you'd like. You can also engage with other YouTubers by commenting or liking and sharing videos.

2. Measurable Analytics

On a high level, the YouTube view counter gives you a good idea of the success of your video. If your view count is in the hundreds of thousands or even millions, you've got a viral video on your hands. Like many social media platforms, YouTube's analytics let you do deeper tracking. There, you can review where your viewers came from, and even see which country likes your videos the most.

3. Huge Audience (and Less Competition)

Millions of people watch YouTube each day. If you craft a short but compelling video, you could get new customers. The audience potential on YouTube alone is huge. When you share your video on other social media platforms as part of a robust social content strategy, the numbers only go up.

Also, not as many companies have dipped their respective toes into videomaking compared to most forms of social networking. That means fewer companies are competing for customer attention. Bigger pond, less fish.

Disadvantages of YouTube Marketing

1. Unprofessional Reputation

We mentioned it before, but it bears repeating: YouTube is still mostly known as a means to kill time. The platform doesn't have the most professional reputation. That's changed somewhat with YouTube Red, and it should continue to change in the future.

2. Commenting Free-for-All

YouTube comment wars erupt on many videos,

especially popular ones. If your video does go viral, your comments section could be hijacked by those who want attention. Comments can sometimes turn sexual and violent. You certainly don't want your company associated with that.

Leveraging the Advantages

YouTube can be a valuable tool, especially when used with other social media marketing. Here are some tips for leveraging YouTube to your advantage:

• Make high-quality videos with professional equipment and lighting

• Keep your videos short to maintain interest

• Monitor comments and respond quickly when appropriate

• Use YouTube analytics to track short-term and long-term marketing success

If you need some help creating a successful YouTube marketing campaign or want help monitoring your online reputation, you can contact any firm that does!

CHAPTER 2

GUIDE TO YOUTUBE MARKETING

If I ask you compile a list right now of social media channels, from the most important to the least important, which would rank at the top? For almost everyone, that answer would be Facebook.

Now another question—which would be at the bottom? For a large number of businesses (and I mean a lot), that would probably be YouTube.

Wrong! Because YouTube can do a lot for the businesses who utilize it correctly and consistently.

In order to do this, you need to understand how YouTube marketing is different than other social channels and how to use that to your advantage.

This guide is beginner friendly - because it can help you build your YouTube channel from the ground up, but it also provides an advanced marketing strategy that everyone can benefit from.

In this paper, I'll go over setting up your channel, optimizing and editing your videos, how to think outside the box with new strategies, monetization, and how to advertise on YouTube.

If you want to know how to use YouTube to market your business, this eBook is for you!

Ready to dive in?

Let's get started.

YOUTUBE MARKETING: THE BASICS

Before we get to the how-to, let's cover the basics that everyone should know before they get started on the actual platform. Trust me, you don't want to skip this section even if you've already got a channel up and running.

Why You Should Be Marketing On YouTube

It only makes sense that before we dive into how

you can grow your channel, we'll cover why you would want to do so. There's plenty of great benefits to marketing on YouTube that many businesses don't fully consider.

The first is nearly self-explanatory. Video is huge right now. It is dominating the world of marketing, and if you aren't using video, you'll almost certainly lose out to your competitors. That's not a hyperbole; with video ranking higher on all social platforms and performing well in ads, customers are more likely to notice and respond to businesses using video.

When you're using YouTube, you'll have a whole library of videos. You can then upload the video files natively to each platform. You can also embed the YouTube videos into your blog posts with just a few clicks, making your blog posts more dynamic and engaging.

YouTube also has an enormous and very diverse audience, which happily uses both YouTube's and Google's own search engine to find content they're looking for. If you're able to optimize for the right keywords (and I'll show you how to do that later in this guide!), you'll be able to connect with that audience instantly, instead of hoping a Facebook Ad shows up in their feed. This allows them to find also has an enormous and very diverse audience, which happily uses both YouTube's and Google's own search engine to find content they're looking for. If you're able to optimize for the right keywords (and I'll show you how to do that later in this guide!), you'll be able to connect with that audience instantly, instead of hoping a Facebook Ad shows up in their feed. This allows them to find you, not the other way around.

Since YouTube videos can show up early on in Google's search results and YouTube is the second most commonly-used search engine after Google, you want to have this huge benefit on your side.

One last benefit? Only 9% of small businesses are using YouTube. You'll have less industry competition here than any other platform, giving you an edge.

YouTube Demographics

When I say YouTube has a large and diverse audience, I mean it. They have 1,300,000 active users, and the site gets over 30 million visitors every single day. We know that YouTube's audience watches more than 3.25 billion hours of video every month, and more than 1 billion video views every single day. That's a heck of a lot of video.

But what about the audience themselves? According to research. here's what we know:

• 11% of YouTube's audience is 18-24

• 23% are ages 25-34

• 26% are 35-44

• 16% are 45-54

• 8% are 50-64

• 3% are 65+

• 14% are undetermined

Since we know that 8 out of 10 people between the ages of 18-49 watch YouTube at least once per month, that gives you an enormous audience waiting to see what you have to offer.

We also know that mobile video views are increasing across all platforms, but that this is especially true for YouTube—and that users here are willing to stick around a little longer; the average mobile viewing session lasts about 40 minutes on YouTube, which is substantial. So, when creating your content, keep mobile viewers in mind.

YouTube: Unlike Any Other Social Channels

In order to truly succeed on YouTube, you need to approach it differently than other social platforms. Facebook, Instagram, and Twitter revolve around both creating and sharing great content with the goal of creating awareness, engagement, and conversation. (That's a simple definition, but for the purpose of this argument, it will work for now).

It's about actually socializing.

I do not think this is how most people use YouTube. YouTube videos are more like blog posts and fit more effectively into the niche of content marketing. Sure, people will comment— but they do so in a manner similar to how they comment on blog posts. They come to view and digest videos, not necessarily share their thoughts about the day. Because of this, you should approach YouTube as content marketing instead of social media marketing.

Some key differences to highlight this:

• People are most likely to find your videos on YouTube The by searching for them, or when viewing other relevant content. On most social media sites (Pinterest being the exception) they'll see you from ads, if they're following you, or from engagement of a friend on your content.

• The emphasis of YouTube is on watching videos, not discussing them. You don't really see people tagging each other in the comments like you do on other sites. It's about the viewer's experience, not a social one. If people want to do this, they'll share the video onto their own social platforms

• Many people come to YouTube with the intention of sitting down and watching some serious video. They don't necessarily get on idly and scroll through a feed the same way they do on Facebook.

By approaching YouTube as a platform for content instead of a social one, you can create stronger videos that will perform well.

YouTube Updates

This is the last thing we need to cover before jumping into the how-to, but it's an important section. YouTube has recently made some changes on the site, and it's important to address them so we're all on the same page.

I'll discuss many of these updates within this post, but here are some of the most important ones to note:

• Mobile users can speed up or slow down videos

• YouTube is currently working on a way to seamlessly adapt videos to any screen, making the platform more mobile-friendly

• There has been an overhaul in ad content lately, due to controversy when ads were being shown on videos that contained extremism, hate speech, and other content businesses did not want to be associated with. Now, channels of arms dealers, political commentators, and even video games have seen fewer ads on their content. This only really affects those who are trying to monetize their YouTube by placing ads on their site, not so much for those running the ads.

• You now need 10,000 views on your channel before you can apply for monetization. For small businesses looking to use YouTube as "passive income," this will pose a challenge. Most businesses, however, benefit most from using YouTube for content marketing purposes, so this won't affect many of the people reading this post.

• Last year, in case you missed it, YouTube

improved their comment moderation tools, making it easier for channels to weed out or prevent comments containing certain phrases or words from being able to appear on their videos. You can read more about comment moderation here.

And now, we're done with the basics. Let's get right into YouTube marketing, starting with how to optimize your channel.

HOW TO OPTIMIZE YOUR YOUTUBE CHANNEL

I firmly believe that every business should optimize their channel before they even post the first video. If you already have your channel up and running, though, it's never too late to make some edits.

Even if you have already set up a channel, you may

find this section of the eBook useful. Go through the following list and make sure you've ticked all the boxes. This will ensure you've used good SEO tactics throughout your account, giving you strong foundations for your YouTube marketing.

1. Create a Brand Account on YouTube

It is a good idea to set up a YouTube channel that is made specifically for your brand. This may seem like an obvious step when it comes to creating a channel for a company, but even one-person businesses should consider setting up an account that is designated to the brand and not to the individual.

Let's say you make cakes for a living, and you want to promote your business and make some extra money by sharing cake decorating tips on YouTube. Which account name do you think will work better — your name ("Jane Doe"), or a brand name (such as "Cakes By Jane")?

Creating a YouTube channel specifically for your business will improve brand visibility and help people to recognize you as an authority in your industry. Plus, a brand account can allow multiple people to contribute to the channel from their Google Accounts.

Do you have a personal account but need to start a brand account? You can either create a new channel, or move your existing one to a brand account.

2. Customize channel icon and channel art

The channel icon and cover art will be two of the first things a visitor will notice about your brand on YouTube. It is essential that we personalize both of these things to better reflect your brand and connect with viewers.

The channel icon is the small image that appears on your channel, with your comments and so on. It works similar to a Facebook profile picture. YouTube recommends using an image at 800 x 800 pixels.

For a business account, I suggest you upload either

a high-res version of your brand logo or a professional headshot of yourself. Try to use the same (or similar) images on your other social media accounts for instant brand recognition.

Next, we want to customize your channel artwork.

Choose an image that communicates who you are as a business, while also being visually engaging. YouTube recommends uploading your cover photo at 2560 x 1440 pixels with a maximum file size of 4MB.

Keep in mind that your channel art will appear differently on each device (computer, TV, and mobile). Check that the main components of your cover art (such as logo, taglines, and text) remain visible; YouTube makes this easy with a preview tool when you upload your image.

Customize your YouTube channel with branded cover art.

3. Write a channel description

Don't ignore this oft-overlooked step! A well-written channel description can be an amazing selling point for your brand.

Think of the channel description as an autobiography for your business. Tell viewers who you are, what you do, and — most importantly — what value you can bring to them. That's your main goal. Write a channel description that demonstrates to users why they should watch your videos and subscribe to your channel.

Your channel description can include useful information like your email address, your location, or links to your website or social media accounts.

4. Add links

YouTube marketing will not only promote the content on your channel but your brand as a whole. Make it easy for viewers to become long-term followers of your brand by adding direct access to your other social channels.

Any links you add will appear prominently in the bottom right-hand corner of your cover art. You can add up to five custom links, which could take users to your website, social media networks, merchandise providers, and more.

These links are easy to see and highly clickable, so be sure to choose the marketing avenues that are most important for the communication between your business and your audience.

Add important links to your YouTube channel art to improve engagement.

5. Create a channel trailer/featured video

Optimize your channel for "new visitors" or for "returning subscribers" by adding a channel trailer and featured video, respectively.

Channel trailers are autoplay videos that (like a good movie trailer) will hook the viewer in and make them want to see more. Create a channel trailer that is short and sweet. Give viewers a quick insight into your brand, your style, and the types of topics you cover.

Users who have already subscribed, however, will

not see your channel trailer. Instead, use a featured video to promote a new video, popular content, or a video that best captures the soul of your brand.

So, have you ticked those five things off your channel to-do list? Excellent! Now it's time to explore the YouTube SEO practices that we need to be using when we upload videos.

Produce Optimized Video Content

We've just optimized the heck out of your YouTube channel. But it doesn't stop there! A crucial part of YouTube marketing is using good SEO practices to optimize your videos and improve your search rankings.

We'll look at this in two parts:

• Creating the content (how do I produce engaging videos that my viewers want to see?)

• Uploading the content (how do I optimize my videos for search?)

CREATING THE CONTENT

1. Do your research

You want the videos you create to bring value to your audience. This could mean providing entertainment, supplying information, showing a step-by-step tutorial, or anything else that satisfies a need.

Research is a vital part of YouTube marketing. This will help you to produce the types of videos that your audience is interested in, and ultimately improve your view rates. Here are a few different ways to identify effective topics for your content:

- Check out your competition

A good way to research topic ideas is by scoping your competition. This isn't about plagiarizing or blindly mimicking another channel's content. After all, how could you ever stand out from the crowd if you never break the mold?

Nevertheless, remaining aware of what your competitors are doing can provide useful groundwork for your own content. Take an inventory of the most popular channels and videos in your industry, and identify ways that you can bring a fresh new take on existing topics.

- Use Google Trends

Google Trends is an amazing place to find ideas for video topics (as well as identify tags and keywords we can use when we upload the video). The advantage here is that creating a video based on a trending topic will benefit from the natural flow of search intent that already exists.

The Google Trends homepage will show a list of the day's top trending topics. Alternatively, you can enter a search term. This will present you with a graph, which shows how often that keyword, subject or phrase has been queried over time, plus a map of the top countries interested in that term.

Google Trends will help you identify popular trends and topics for your YouTube marketing.

- Keyword research

One last tool that will help you is the Google Adwords Keyword Planner. This tool will help you reach the right customers with the right keywords, and give you ideas about what people are typing in when they want to find your videos.

The "Find Keywords" page of AdWords will show variations of any keyword you enter, supplying alternate ideas for your content. To improve your visibility, look for keywords with high search volume (which means people are looking for these topics) and low competition (which means their needs aren't yet being met by your competitors).

You can also see what words people are using to find your channel in the YouTube Analytics Traffic Sources report (Analytics > Traffic Sources > YouTube Search). You could incorporate the most relevant search terms for your video's metadata, or use them as inspiration for your new videos.

For instance, say you are a fitness trainer who

provides workout videos. You notice that a prominent traffic source for your channel is people searching for "5-minute workouts". Using this insight, you could now create an entire playlist of different five-minute workout routines.

These videos will be highly searchable, allowing you to meet the existing needs of your audience and grow your viewership.

2. Find your point of difference

There are a lot of users on YouTube. How do you make your voice stand out?

My best advice is to stick to your passions.

Some creators become so fixated on the idea of gaining hundreds of subscribers or making money on YouTube that they lose sight of the value that they intended to bring to their audience.

It's okay to want to grow your viewership and earn money with your YouTube channel (who doesn't want that?), but look beyond that.

YouTube success is often achieved by creators who produce passionate content for a niche community. When viewers finally find a channel that caters to their unique interests, they respond with enthusiasm.

That means more views, engagement, and watch time for you.

Get to know your audience, tap into a niche market, and make the videos you enjoy creating.

3. Diversify your video content

There are many different types of videos. While you don't want to confuse viewers by radically changing your style and format each time, you may find that diversifying your content can help keep subscribers interested in your channel.

Some popular video types include:

- Explainer videos & tutorials

Explainer videos are a great way to establish your

brand as an authority. Answer customer questions, provide information and create value through the acquisition of knowledge.

- **Customer testimonials**

Reach out to satisfied customers and see if anyone is willing to participate in a short-form interview. Customer testimonials can improve the credibility and brand loyalty of your business.

- *Product demonstrations*

Has your business started selling a new product? Do you want to showcase your range? Use YouTube marketing to demonstrate the benefits of your products. All the better if you can include positive customer reviews!

- *Vlogs (video blogs)*

With videos about gaming, fitness, cooking, or simply daily life, it is safe to say that vlogs are very popular on YouTube. Creating vlogs means going up against a lot of competition, but there is also a lot of potential for creativity with this video type.

- *YouTube Live*

Broadcasting live videos on YouTube allows you to create a direct and unfiltered line of communication with your audience.

This is great for Q&A sessions, or for establishing a rapport with viewers. Learn how to start a YouTube live stream here.

Communicate directly with your viewers using YouTube Live.

Some video types will be more useful for your business than others. Before filming any video, ask yourself: what do I want to achieve with my YouTube marketing? Identify specific goals (lead generation, sales, brand visibility, etc.) and choose video types that are best suited to accomplish them.

UPLOADING THE CONTENT

1. Use keywords in your title

The next step to becoming a YouTube marketing pro is to optimize your video's metadata. This means giving your viewers (as well as YouTube's search and discovery system) the information they need to be able to find your content.

First up is the title of your video.

The title is the first thing people will read as they scroll through their search results. It could mean the difference between someone clicking your video or the one underneath it. Here are a few quick tips on how to write good video titles:

• Make sure your titles are no longer than 60-70 characters to prevent text being truncated in results pages.

• Include important keywords — and where possible, put them at the beginning of your title for extra emphasis.

• Spark curiosity with a creative title, but make sure it honestly describes or hints at the video's content. Avoid using inaccurate or clickbait titles;

these tactics can lead to a higher bounce rate and lower rankings!

Put some thought into the titles of your videos. They are an important piece of metadata that can attract more viewers to your channel

and build anticipation for your content.

2. Write a compelling description

Descriptions are a critical source of information for YouTube's search system. Writing keyword-rich video descriptions will help viewers find the content they want to watch. It will also improving the video's discoverability on YouTube.

Keep these tips in mind when writing your video description:

•   YouTube will show the first two or three lines of your description, and then viewers will need to click "show more." For this reason, you'll want to prioritize the most important information (keywords, CTAs, important links) at the beginning of the description.

• Remember Google Trends? This tool will come in handy again here. Use it to choose relevant keywords and phrases that have a high level of interest to maximize traffic from search results.

• Avoid keyword stuffing. You want the description to read naturally. Too many keywords, may make your content appear "spammy." Try reading the description out loud to see if you've used coherent sentences.

• Some creators like to include a video transcript in the description (either verbatim or as a shortened version). Your video content is likely full of natural keywords, so you may find this strategy useful for striking the right balance.

• Include links to your website, social channels, blog posts, or to video-specific time stamps to encourage people to interact with your content, both on and off YouTube.

Whatever you do, don't leave the description field blank. Writing searchable descriptions is crucial for YouTube marketing, as they can significantly boost views and watch time for your channel.

3. Choose the right tags

Say it again: keywords! Write tags to highlight your main keywords and improve the visibility of your video. Think about the phrases people might use if they were searching for videos like yours. Try to include a mix of short keywords and long-tail keywords to broaden the video's reach.

Optimize your YouTube videos by writing keyword-rich titles, descriptions, and tags.

4. Create custom thumbnails

Your video thumbnail is the image people see when scrolling through the search results. When done well, the thumbnail can greatly improve the click-through rate of your video.

When you upload a video, YouTube will provide you with a few auto-generated thumbnail options. You may be able to use one of those, especially when you're just started out. But we highly recommend you upload your own customized thumbnail to stand out on the search engine results page.

According to YouTube, 90 percent of the best performing videos have custom thumbnails. Create a more polished look for your content by using clear imagery and key information. It can be a good idea to include your logo or your headshot to allow for instant recognition of your brand.

Remember that around half of your audience will be viewing your channel on a mobile. Check that your thumbnail is visible on all devices and external sites that embed YouTube videos.

Please note that you will first need to verify your YouTube account to upload custom thumbnail images. Simply visit youtube.com/verify to receive a verification code.

5. Include CTAs

CTAs, or calls-to-action, are images, buttons, or other prompts that elicit action from your viewers. With effective CTAs, you can improve conversion rates by compelling your audience to perform a desired task. These tasks could include subscribing to your YouTube channel, making a purchase, visiting your website and so on.

Here are a few ways to include CTAs and add interactivity to your YouTube marketing:

• Deliver a verbal call-to-action at the end of each video you film. Try something like, "Thank you for watching! If you want to learn more about [blank], head to my website or check out my other videos." The goal is to drive engagement and keep viewers informed.

• Include sponsored cards on your YouTube videos. These small CTA pop-ups can simplify the discovery process for users by providing immediate access to your other relevant videos, or a link to your website, online shop or so on.

• Add call-to-action overlays to your videos. These appear as unobtrusive, semi-transparent banners in the lower left corner of the videos. If your goal is to increase traffic to your website, a

CTA overlay ad will be extremely helpful.

• Use the video description to prompt action from your audience. Try to put the most important CTAs and links at the beginning of the description (so they will be visible before the "Show more" cutoff), then another at the end.

CTAs are an important part of YouTube marketing. Try using sponsored cards!

So now you know some of the most important tactics for YouTube marketing — how to optimize your YouTube channel, and how to optimize each individual video. These steps are the foundation of all good YouTube marketing. But there are other strategies you can use to grow your channel, attract subscribers and become a YouTube pro.

HOW TO PROMOTE YOUR YOUTUBE CONTENT

Now that you've produced a video and optimized it for search let's talk about how to market your

YouTube channel and videos. While ranking high in search results and having a large subscriber base are ideal, those goals can be difficult to achieve when you're just starting out.

That's why it's important to always spread the word about your YouTube channel and videos across other platforms. Fortunately, YouTube, and other platforms make it easy to share video content.

Below are some tips for how to best promote your YouTube content on other channels:

- **Social Media**

Sharing your videos on social is an easy way to add additional insights to your video and engage with viewers. YouTube makes it incredibly simple for you and others to promote your video across other social networks. To share a video, just click the "Share" tab underneath the video. There you can select where to market the video. YouTube even provides a shortened URL to your video for convenient posting.

When promoting your YouTube channel or videos on your social media sites, consider the best marketing strategy. Simply sharing the video on your timeline or feed may not be the most effective option. Think of why you made the video. Maybe you created a tutorial because users were asking a lot of questions about how to use your product.

In that case, it might be best to respond to those questions with a link to your video. If you created a video as part of a larger campaign or global trend, be sure to include relevant #hashtags where appropriate to ensure your video is included in the conversation. If you created a video to build awareness around your brand, consider posting the link in your profile bios.

- **Blog Posts and Website**

Market your YouTube channel and videos on your website and blog. First, add a YouTube follow icon to your website and blog, so your audience can easily find your channel. Second, embed relevant videos on your website or in blog posts. Consider creating a YouTube video to accompany a specific blog post or sharing customer video reviews or case studies on your website. Not only will this help market your YouTube channel and videos, but it will also drive traffic to your website.

- Email

While you're on the quest to find and attract new customers and leads, don't forget about the ones you already have. Share your video content and channel with relevant email lists. Encourage your contacts to check out a blog post you've in which embedded a video to increase both the video and website traffic or direct them to a relevant playlist you've curated. Sending an email newsletter with valuable information and video content is another great way to keep your contacts engaged.

- Q&A Sites

Do your videos help solve a problem or answer a question? If so, engaging with popular Q&A sites like Quora might be a great marketing technique for your business. Monitor questions and share video content users will find helpful.

- Collaborate With Others

Does your company have a relationship with another company that has a great YouTube presence? Ask them to collaborate! Collaborating with others is a fun way for both channels to gain exposure to another audience. Create a video or playlist together. There are a lot of options to creatively collaborate with other brands, just make sure that their audience and goal is similar to yours. The partnership should align with your marketing strategy.

- Engage With Viewers

Finally, be sure to engage with your viewers. Respond to comments, answer questions, ask for feedback, and thank viewers for their support. This is an easy task to forget or let fall by the wayside so try to choose a dedicated time to check video interactions and respond to users.

Essential Tips to Market Your YouTube Channel and Videos

Above, we touched on some components to build a high-level marketing strategy for your YouTube videos. In this section, we're going to discuss some tips for how to best promote your YouTube content.

1. Keep your channel branding consistent with your other social media accounts

2. Optimize your title and description for SEO and searcher intent

3. Feature real people or animated faces in your videos, not just words or B-roll

4. Choose a video thumbnail that accurately represents your video content

5. Include calls-to-action (CTAs) in every video

6. Make it easy for others to share your videos

7. Create playlists that feature your videos and others

8. Produce videos on a regular basis, and consider doing a video series

UNDERSTANDING YOUTUBE ANALYTICS FOR YOUR BUSINESS

You've put a lot of time and effort into your YouTube channel. You've created interesting content, optimized it for SEO, and shared it across different platforms … now it's time to measure your success.

YouTube Analytics can seem daunting at first. Let's face it, interpreting a bunch of numbers and strange looking graphs can be pretty challenging. Thankfully, understanding YouTube Analytics is pretty straightforward once you know your way around.

- Determine Your Goal

First things first, you can't measure your success without determining your goal. If you've filmed, edited, uploaded, optimized, and shared your video and still don't know what goal you're trying to achieve, we have an issue. Your goal should drive your video strategy from beginning to end.

You should focus on targeting one goal per video (as we talk about here). Some of the most common video goals are to increase brand awareness, views, clicks, or inbound links or social shares. Depending on how you use the video in your marketing material, the goal could be to increase the open rate of an email series or improve the conversion rate on a landing page. YouTube is a great platform for growing brand awareness.

As the world's second largest search engine, YouTube allows your videos to be seen through organic search or paid advertising. Video is a great way to humanize your brand by showcasing real employees, customers, or partners. It also allows you to build credibility by publishing informational content that helps your target buyer. Promoting your videos through paid advertising versus organic search can impact the type of video you should create. If you're planning to increase awareness organically, consider filming the history of your company, customer reviews, or product tutorials.

- Key Metrics to Track

Now that we've talked about why determining a goal is so important, we can discuss how to effectively measure success. At first glance, YouTube analytics can be pretty overwhelming. On the flip side, it's frustrating when you post a video and don't receive as many views or as much engagement as you were expecting. YouTube analytics shows you how viewers found your content, how long they watched it, and how much they engaged with it. Let's start by going over what exactly you can measure and how to find it.

First, head to youtube.com/analytics. You should be directed to an analytics dashboard that shows an overview of how your videos have been performing during the past 28 days. You can adjust the analytics timeframe by clicking on the drop-down menu in the upper right-hand corner. The overview report features some top-line performance metrics, engagement metrics, demographics, traffic sources, and popular content.

You can also filter your results by content, device type, geography or location, all video content or playlists, subscriber status, playback type, traffic by different YouTube products, and translations. In addition, to filtering results, YouTube allows you to display your results in a variety of different charts and even an interactive map.

While there's no one-size-fits-all approach for reporting and measuring the success of a campaign, below are a few key metrics that you should pay attention to.

- Watch Time and Audience Retention

Watch time reports the total number of minutes your audience has spent viewing your content on your channel as a whole and by video. This helps you see what pieces of content viewers are actually consuming instead of just clicking on and navigating away from.

Watch time is important because it's one of YouTube's ranking factors. A video with a higher watch time is more likely to rank higher in results. YouTube provides a line item report on watch time, views, average view duration, and average percentage viewed for individual videos, location, publish date, and more.

A video's average percentage viewed, or retention rate, indicates the average percentage of a video your audience watches per view. A higher percentage means there's a higher chance that your audience will watch that video until the end. Try placing cards and end screens in videos with a higher average percentage viewed rate to improve the number of views your calls-to-action receive.

- **Traffic Sources**

The traffic sources report shows how viewers are finding your content online. This provides valuable insight on where to best promote your YouTube content. For example, you can see if viewers are finding your content through YouTube search or Twitter. To view more in-depth traffic reporting, click on the overall traffic source category. This data can help refine your YouTube marketing strategy. Be sure to optimize your metadata based on your findings.

- Demographics

The demographics report helps you understand your audience by reporting on their age and gender. You can then break down age groups and genders by other criteria such as geography. This report will help you better market to your YouTube audience and understand if your content is resonating with your established buyer personas.

- Engagement Reports

Engagement reports help you learn what content is resonating with your audience. Here you can see what viewers are clicking, sharing, commenting, and promoting. You can also see how your cards and end screens are performing in your engagement reports. Cards and end screens reports help you learn what your audience is engaging with so you can optimize your calls-to-action in future videos.

YOUTUBE SEO: BEST PRACTICES

If there's one thing that you take away from this 4,000+ word guide, let it be this section. You should optimize the heck out of your YouTube videos for SEO. I explained why you should do this early on, with YouTube and Google's searches being a powerful factor in which videos get more views.

YouTube SEO shares many of the same fundamental principles as on-page optimization. You should be optimizing your videos for search in several ways:

• Add the highest-ranking keywords to the title

• Place additional keywords in the video description

• Choose the right tags for your videos, so they will show up in relevant search engines

You don't have to choose between a catchy video title and a keyword-laden one, for what it's worth. Plenty of great videos (that rank really well) use the strategy of choosing a catchy title, and then adding a colon and placing the keyword title afterwards. An example can be seen here:

When writing your description, you can try to optimize for the top keywords, but also additional keywords that you think could be helpful. In the video above, you can see that the description has keywords like "rainbow unicorn cake" and "classic rainbow cake." Both of these may be search terms, and they have their bases covered.

When researching keywords, I recommend doing keyword research both for Google, and specifically for YouTube. This way, you'll make sure that you're ranking as best you can on both search engines, increasing views significantly. Any of the top keyword research tools will work for Google (I discuss them in-depth here), and I most recommend keywordtool.io's YouTube-specific search. Prioritize the keywords you find in the YouTube search, as this will be your best bet for being found.

HOW TO CREATE VIDEOS THAT CONVERT

Ultimately, none of what we've discussed so far matters much if your videos suck. Whether the content is bad or they just aren't actionable, videos that are incapable of driving results just waste your time and money. When creating videos for YouTube, focus on specific goals. For many businesses, that will be lead generation and sales.

There's several strategies you can use to create videos that are more successful at converting.

These include:

- Creating videos that you know will be searched for by members of your target audience, organizing them into a playlist, and placing a CTA at the end to learn more, either through a lead magnet or by contacting you.

- Organizing videos into playlists which act as a funnel that push towards conversions; users are more likely to convert from you after several videos instead of just one

- Creating videos that offer your product as a solution to a customer's problem

There's a lot of room to get creative with strategies here. The key is, though, to focus on specific goals and create videos to accomplish them; not the other way around. Keep the digital sales funnel in mind, just like you would on your blog, and nudge users towards conversion accordingly.

YOUTUBE MONETIZATION

When I'm asked "Should I monetize my channel?"

by a client, I always ask "do you mean monetize like show ads and try to get paid?" For most businesses, I do not recommend that course of action. I have a few good reasons why.

The first is that viewer attention spans- and loyalty- are a bitch. I'm even lumping in my own impatience online here; as a user, if I click to watch a tutorial, an ad pops up, and I see a similar tutorial in the "You May Also Like This" feed, I'll give that one a shot instead. I'm not kidding. I've done this twice today. You don't want to do anything that will cause viewers to lose interest in your video, or worse, to click to a competitor's video instead.

YouTube ads are more beneficial for the advertiser than the owner of the videos the ads are playing on in most cases.

Plus, the money you'll make as a result of these monetization options isn't exactly going to be sending you into early retirement. You might make something like $1 per 1,000 views, and you can't even get paid until you hit the $100 mark. For most businesses, this takes ages. Many find that it's not worth the risk of losing viewers for pennies of potential profit.

The goal for most businesses on YouTube is to monetize through soft-selling and lead generation, not actual pay-per-video-view ads. Focus on this strategy, which we've discussed how to do in other sections, and you'll make much more profit from YouTube than by running ads on your videos.

The two exceptions here are:

\- If you've built up a large subscriber base who you know will happily wait through the ads for your content.

\- If your business is becoming semi-famous on YouTube. Still, for the latter, wait until you have at least 5-10 thousand subscribers before enabling ads.

How to Monetize YouTube

If you decide that monetization is the right choice

for your business and/or that you vehemently disagree with me, here's how to monetize YouTube videos.

Go to your Creator's Studio, and then click on the Channel tab. You'll see the monetization box, where it says "Enable." Click on it.

You'll see the requirements that YouTube has. **These are:**

• You've accepted the YouTube partner terms

• You've requested access to AdSense

• You set your monetization preferences

• Your channel has had 10,000 views

While you need at least 10,000 views to be able to monetize the account, you can start the submission process before that. There's a good chance that you've already accepted YouTube partner terms when creating your account, and that you have AdSense access for your site.

When you set your monetization preferences,

you'll see several options. Select the ones you'd want to use and hit "save." *These include:*

• Display ads (desktop only), which you must select to monetize. These appear above the "what you might like to watch" videos.

• Overlay ads, which are desktop only and show up as a small overlay in front of your videos.

• Sponsored cards, which can be shown to users on all devices, and will appear to the side of your videos.

• Skippable video ads, which play before your video and will be shown to both desktop and mobile users.

Once your channel gets 10,000 views, you'll start earning money on video views if it is approved. Make sure your account is in good standing and following community guidelines.

HOW TO ADVERTISE ON YOUTUBE

What if you want to be on the other side of the

monetization- if you want to use ads to promote your business, instead of profiting from views of said ads? This is something I can happily recommend for businesses. Here's how to advertise on YouTube:

- To get started, YouTube Ads are actually run through Google Adwords, so if you don't have an account already, they'll have you create an account. Once, you do this, click "Start Now."

- The YouTube/Adwords ad creator looks a little different than what Facebook/Pinterest/Twitter/Quora ads managers look like. They display all four creation steps on a page, and you click on each in order to add and edit the content there. First, select your video.

- You can search for the title or URL of the YouTube video that you want to promote.

- Next, add in your ad text and choose your Thumbnail. Remember that this text is designed purely to act as a CTA; it doesn't need to be a video title or description.

- Decide where you want to send users who click the ad. You can send them to your channel, or to your site. In the majority of cases, sending viewers to your site will be the most beneficial.

- Next, set your budget and your maximum CPC (optional). YouTube Ads work on a bidding system like all other PPC systems, and you'll only pay when viewers view the ad.

- The last step here is particularly crucial: the targeting section of the campaign creation. You can target based on location, gender, age group, their web activity, and interests. Take all of these into consideration; interest targeting is perhaps even more important here than it is on Facebook Ads.

Once all this is filled out, you'll review the ad an enter in billing information. Then submit!

HOW TO HOST YOUTUBE CONTESTS

We all know about Facebook contests, Instagram contests, and even Pinterest contestshttps://blog.hootsuite.com/secrets-youtube-contest/. But what about YouTube contests? They're not as common, but they are a great strategy. Since they're not as common, this gives you an edge if you decide to use them. Like all other social contests, a YouTube contest can do a lot to help increase subscribers, engagement, and social shares. And, when executed correctly, lead generation and/or user generated content.

Different common types of YouTube contests include:

• Commenting contests, where viewers leave a comment as their entry; this is designed to drive engagement.

• Subscriber contests, where non-subscribers can enter by subscribing to your channel

• Response video contests, where viewers are encouraged to create and upload their own videos in response to yours. By requiring them to make them "response videos," they'll be easier to find.

• Vote contests, where users are asked to vote for their favorite option, similar to the Pinterest concept here. This may take users off the site.

If you want to make lead generation possible with a YouTube contest, you're in luck. ShortStack recently released a new contest software template just for YouTube contests. This template allows you to capture lead information just like you would on Facebook or Instagram contests utilizing the software. Users can actually get entries by voting, or by sharing with their friends. You also have the options that come with the rest of ShortStack software, like setting age limits. If you're going the contest route to boost your strategy and engagement, I recommend testing out the ShortStack templates.

Final Thoughts

YouTube marketing is often completely forgotten about by most businesses, but it could just be the tool you need to set you apart from your competition.

By approaching YouTube as another leg to your content marketing strategy, you'll be able to create great video content that will enhance both content and social media marketing.

Video is the hottest thing in marketing right now, and I don't think that's going away; embrace it by signing up your business for YouTube and diving in today.

CHAPTER 3

YOUTUBE TRICKS AND TIPS

With one billion hours of video watched daily by over one billion users, YouTube seems like an automatic ticket to visibility. But clicking that upload button is just the first step in securing your place as a successful video creator. If you want your videos to meet those eyeballs—and bring in business—you'll need to be smart about your

YouTube marketing:

• Get Discovered

• Gain an Audience

• Automate Your YouTube Marketing

GET DISCOVERED

When you upload videos, YouTube helps you build audiences for those videos by sharing them in various ways:

• **Search results:** All public videos are considered in YouTube's search function. When a user enters a query in the search bar on YouTube, the most relevant results—based on title, tags, and popularity—are displayed.

• **Home screen recommendations:** YouTube's home screen is customized to the tastes of each individual user. So when a user arrives on YouTube, the platform suggests content they might find interesting based on what they've watched in the past.

• **In-video recommendations:** When users watch videos on YouTube, a sidebar appears with recommended videos based on the content of the video they're currently watching as well as other content the user has watched in the past. When the video is over, an end screen appears with additional recommendations.

• Trending videos: YouTube also has a Trending tab that aggregates the most viewed new videos. This feed is mostly reserved for the top channels on the platform—think late night talk show hosts like Jimmy Fallon and successful individual creators like Tati.

Google may be smart, but it can't watch your videos and give them titles and tags...yet. All of the metadata—title, description, tags, thumbnail, and category—has to be created by you, and it will help both YouTube and potential viewers understand what your video is about.

For more tips and tricks, including things like specific dimensions for channel art and character limits for descriptions, head over to the official YouTube course on how to get discovered.

SET YOUR TITLE, DESCRIPTION, TAGS, THUMBNAIL, AND CATEGORY

While some viral videos are able to thrive without these basic elements, fully-outfitted content is always stronger. Head to the "Basic info" tab as you're uploading to get started:

- Create a title

Your title should be short: The limit is 100 characters, but titles start getting cut off in search around 70 characters. The most important part of a title: It needs to actually reflect what your video is about. A jazzy title might be fun, but you want users to find your video when they're searching for specific keywords.

- Write a description

The description provides more detailed information about your video, making it even more searchable while also giving your audience a broader context for what they're watching. In addition to describing the video, it can also link out to relevant content, or even to your social networks.

But be careful about length. While some successful YouTubers, like creator JennaMarbles, write long missives as descriptions, best practice is to keep it short. For the most part, people are on YouTube to watch, not to read. Plus, YouTube truncates descriptions (adding a "Show More" link if users want the whole thing) after about 100 characters. So include the most important information upfront—including links back to your website or social media accounts.

- Pick your tags

Your tags will help YouTube better understand what your video is about. That will help it place your video in relevant searches and as suggestions on other relevant videos. Performing a quick YouTube search for one of the keywords in your title will help you identify more potential tags. For example, if your video is called "How to Use Old Clothes to Make New Styles," you might search the word "clothes" and see what the suggested searches are.

Your suggested searches may include "clothes haul," "clothes hacks," "clothes day," or "clothes shopping." That means people are searching for those terms, but it doesn't mean that you should add all of them. Only add the relevant search terms, or YouTube might dock you in their results or even remove your video completely. Same goes for adding tags into descriptions, which YouTube calls tag-stuffing.

Time spent watching a video is part of YouTube's algorithm. So if your title, tags, description, thumbnail, or category are misleading, it's unlikely that someone who clicks on your video will watch it for very long—once they realize it's not what they were looking for. If people only watch your videos for a few seconds at a time, the algorithm will notice and will demote your video in results.

-   Customize your thumbnail image

Your video's thumbnail image will show up next to your video in search results and recommendations. It won't increase your visibility in search and recommendations, but it might be the difference between a view and someone scrolling right past your video.

You can easily choose from still images pulled directly from your video, or you can design a unique thumbnail with your preferred photo editing tool. Whichever you choose, pick an image that is attractive and indicative of what the video is about. SciShow's channel offers an example of a great combination of clear and concise text and visually interesting imagery.

- Choose a category

Move to the "Advanced settings" tab to choose a category for your video. Properly labeling your video will help the YouTube algorithm get it out to the correct audience through search and recommended videos. Take a look at YouTube's introduction to categories for tips on best practices.

Once you've taken care of these five main forms of metadata, there are many other customizations in the Creator Studio. You can access this by clicking on your channel icon and choosing "Creator Studio." The Creator Studio gives you a more detailed view of each of your videos, with options to add cards and end screens, translations and transcriptions, along with various tools to personalize your channel, interact with your audience, view analytics, and more.

GAIN AN AUDIENCE

Because the YouTube algorithm builds on itself, the more people watching your videos, the more visible your videos become. The metadata you've just created will help your individual videos get discovered, but just like with any business, it's important to have returning customers. In the YouTube world, the key is getting subscribers: people who will come back to see new content as you create it.

Clicking "Subscribe" on a channel—or on a video made for a given channel—means future uploads by that channel will show up on a viewer's home screen, Subscriptions feed, and notifications, providing them up-to-the-minute access to videos as they are uploaded. Seeing your channel's subscriber number rise, YouTube's algorithm will increase the visibility of your videos in both search and recommended videos, which in turn will get you more subscribers…and the cycle continues.

YOUTUBE CHANNELS: YOUR MARKETING HOME BASE

The first step in gaining subscribers is putting some love into your channel.

YouTube channels are the hub for all YouTube marketing. Think of your channel as the home page for your account: Whenever you upload a video to YouTube, it appears on your channel. By hosting all your videos in one place, you're able to attract return viewers and build a community around your videos.

Every YouTube user, whether or not they produce content, is entitled to a YouTube channel. When you sign up for YouTube, you're able to set up and customize a channel for your account. Then, if you choose to upload to YouTube—and make your videos public—they show up on your channel.

Your channel is your brand, and that means sticking with your niche. As you're putting together a content plan, consider how each piece fits into the narrative of your channel. If videos you produce rank highly within your niche, YouTube will be able to target audiences that are interested in similar content—and your channel's overall visibility will increase. Stay focused with the content you create, and as your viewership increases, so will your subscriber numbers.

PERSONALIZE YOUR CHANNEL

There are a few basic ingredients when it comes to personalizing your YouTube channel.

- **Choose a channel name**

Because your channel is your brand, make sure to choose a channel name that matches. Your channel name appears on your channel itself as well as under your video titles in search and recommended videos. It helps viewers associate an individual video with your broader oeuvre of work.

You can have fun with it, but be sure it's descriptive: If you're not Rihanna or Ellen DeGeneres, putting your name in the title probably won't help you much. Your channel name should have personality and be unique—it's worth

Googling to be sure the name you choose isn't already associated with another brand. But don't go so far out on a limb that no one has any idea what your channel is about: The name also needs to be relevant.

Once you've come up with a channel name, head to the Creator Studio, and then choose "Channel" to name your channel.

-   Set your channel icon

You can update your channel icon by navigating to your channel and clicking on your existing icon.

Many creators use an image of themselves as their icon. Alternatively, a logo or design representing your channel can give you recognizable branding. Because it's such a small space, don't try to cram too much in.

 Save the expression for the banner.

-   Set your channel banner

To set your banner, click "Add channel art" or

hover over your existing banner, click the pencil icon in the right corner, and select "Edit channel art."

Because banners are larger, they allow for a lot of creative expression. And because they're front and center on your channel, you want to be sure that they're on brand.

For inspiration, take a look at two very different banner types:

• TripAdvisor does a great job of using evocative imagery related to its brand—and changing it often to keep things fresh. They save their logo for the icon.

• Yelp sticks to a more standard header, using its logo as the centerpiece and sticking to its signature red color. (Note: If you choose to go this route, be sure your logo is right in the center so it doesn't get blocked by social media share buttons or other elements on the page.)

Pro tip: Using the same icon and banner on your

various social media platforms can make it easier for your audience to locate you across the web.

- Add a watermark

You can also incorporate a logo directly into your videos with a branding watermark, which appears on the bottom right corner of all of your videos. This can help with brand consistency and provide a reminder to new viewers whose channel they're on. When a viewer hovers over the watermark, they're prompted to subscribe to your channel. See it in action on Strawburry17's channel.

Just head to the Creator Studio, navigate from "Channel" to "Branding," and then click "Add a watermark."

- Create a channel trailer

When prospective subscribers arrive at your channel, they'll want to know what to expect. You have a few options for how to achieve that:

1.   Write a channel description: Generally a good idea, but remember, YouTubers are around for the

videos, not the text.

2.   Create a unique video that introduces your style of content (channel trailer): Creator Simone Giertz provides a good example of this.

3.   Use a popular or recent video as your channel trailer, like Miranda Sings, does.

From, your channel, click the "Customize Channel" button, where you can choose a video to feature to returning subscribers and select a channel trailer to feature to new visitors.

Ask For Subscribers

In an ideal world, people would subscribe to your channel just because. But in the real world, you need flat out ask. Here are some ways to do it:

• Ask people to subscribe within your video.

• Share subscribe links in your video descriptions, on your website, or on social media.

• Show subscribe links in end screens.

• Incentivize subscriptions with contests.

YouTube creator DisneyKittee employs many of these tips and tricks and has grown her channel's subscriber count into the five figures in just a year on the platform.

Set A Schedule And Upload Frequently

Once you have subscribers, retaining that existing audience plays a big role in increasing your future audience. To make sure your existing viewers keep coming back, you'll want to set a schedule for your uploads.

Whether it's daily, weekly, or somewhere in between, having a regular upload schedule and communicating that schedule with your audience will give them something to anticipate, creating a dedicated subscriber base. Think about it this way: Would you watch your favorite TV show if you had no idea when the next episode would air? Probably not—too much hassle. YouTube viewers act the same way: If they know what's coming up, they'll tune in.

Start The Conversation With Your Audience

Once your videos start getting views, you have the option of utilizing one of the most powerful aspects of YouTube: user engagement. Interacting through the platform can turn viewers into repeat viewers and repeat viewers into subscribers. There are several avenues to help you get started with engagement:

- **Encourage comments**

The comment section of your videos can be used to build a personal connection with viewers. It provides an open forum for your audience to interact with you and other viewers. An easy way to suggest comments is to mention it verbally in your video or recommend it in your video description. Asking your audience to respond to a question in the comments like Zoella does in her videos may be a good place to start.

A heart will appear alongside the comments you

like on your own videos, moving them to a featured section at the top of the comments section. This encouragement can lead to future interactions with viewers who want to have their comments featured.

- **Respond to comments**

Replying to comments your viewers leave will also boost those comments to the featured section. YouTube favors videos with more interactions, so a longer comments section can easily translate to more views.

- **Set up a Q&A**

Be explicit about your comment interactions by setting up a Q&A. You can schedule it in advance for a specific time, or if you don't think you can get a critical mass of people at any given time, do it asynchronously. For example, in Question Tuesday videos on the Vlogbrothers channel, John Green promises to answer questions in the comments.

- Interact in the moment through live streaming

Live streaming allows you to interact with viewers using a side-by-side chat for real-time community engagement. Instead of waiting for comments like you would on an ordinary video, ask viewers questions in the moment and receive instant feedback.

Live streaming is most common for two types of creators: gamers and nonprofits. Take a look at Jacksepticeye's charity livestream as an example of hitting both those marks at once.

To start a live stream, choose the "Go live" option instead of the regular upload button. And once the live stream is complete, make sure to keep the full live video (as well as the live chat log) archived to your channel.

Don't forget social media. Cross-promotion between YouTube and other social platforms can actually increase your audience interactions. Adding links to your social accounts on YouTube and then posting to social media with channel updates keeps viewers in the know on your latest uploads.

Automate Your YouTube Marketing

Getting discovered and growing your audience isn't easy—it can take hours of tedious data entry and tweaking to get it just right. If it gets to the point where your marketing time is cutting into time you should be spending creating great video content, it's time to automate.

• Promote your YouTube channel without increasing your time spent cross-posting on social networks

• Upload videos to YouTube whenever you save them to your cloud storage

CHAPTER 4

YOUTUBE MARKETING FOR SMALL BUSINESSES

Are you looking for alternative ways to promote your business online? Look no further: YouTube is one of the biggest, most popular websites in the world, which is what makes it an incredibly powerful marketing tool.

Using YouTube marketing for small businesses is the way forward and in fact this is a means that goes beyond just some teens making use of videos to share their exploits and it is also beyond seeing authors who use videos to showcase their book trailers. With the help of well made videos it is now possible to offer very cheap and even free opportunities to small businesses to effectively promote their businesses and also help make their businesses run more smoothly.

A typical use for video marketing for small businesses can be seen in the case of home organizer entrepreneurs that wish to improve their client base in metropolitan areas. As everyone knows, a picture can say and depict far more than a thousand words; so, why not make use of a video to get your message across?

This is certainly a good idea because a persons primitive brain that makes decisions for most of us will do so on the basis of contrasting options. It has in fact been found that video images and also pictures make a significant impact on this primitive brain. In fact, even a short video which may for example depict a customer that seems satisfied will give a clearer picture than any content based message.

In order to use video marketing you can create your own video and also upload it at no cost at a free video sharing website of which YouTube is a good example. Then it is necessary that you send out links to this video to all your customers and in addition you can upload the video at your website and in this way help get the message across very easily.

However, there are also many entrepreneurs that are still skeptical about using video marketing but this is because they have not understood the benefits that can be derived from using this medium to grow a small business. All that is required is understanding the steps that need to be taken to help ensure that your videos get better rankings on, for example, YouTube searches. The same holds true in the case of Google as well.

Remember that like with any other kind of web based content you should not expect success by simply putting up the video on places like YouTube and do nothing more. You must also expend a lot of effort so as to increase brand awareness and also learn how to get more convert their viewing of your videos into sales. Only then can you get the results that will make video marketing worthwhile

Is YouTube marketing the right solution for your business?

As I mentioned, YouTube is one of the biggest websites around – to be more specific, it's currently the second most popular website in the world. And even though most people don't think of YouTube primarily as a search engine, that's exactly what most visitors do on the site. YouTube's not just the second most popular website; it's also the second most popular search engine – topped only by Google. This means that the platform presents a huge potential for reach for your business.

The fact that YouTube is such a hugely popular platform also means that there is a lot of competition. According to Statista, as of July 2015, 400 hours of video are uploaded to YouTube every minute. So, if you want to be successful on

YouTube, you need to make sure that you have the time and the resources to publish quality content on a consistent basis. In other words, you'll need a good YouTube marketing plan.

Another big reason why YouTube is such an attractive option for marketing purposes is that it's all about video – and video marketing is all the rage right now. Video has consistently proven itself as one of the best-performing forms of contentin terms of engagement, and just because you're creating them for YouTube doesn't mean that you can't repurpose your videos. These videos would be great for your other social profiles, your email marketing campaigns, your website and landing pages, and any other platforms or channels you might be using.

As for the issue of video production, it's not as difficult as it may seem to create marketing videos. You don't need a huge budget and you don't even need to make substantial investments in equipment – but we'll discuss video production and all that it entails further on in this guide.

So, the short of it: is YouTube the right solution for your business? Yes, in most cases. If you sell products, it's a great way to showcase and promote them and all of their uses. If you're a B2B company, it's a great platform for expanding your reach and for generating more leads.

Developing A Youtube Marketing Strategy

Marketing on YouTube is like marketing on other social platforms: the first step is to create your strategy. In order to create your YouTube marketing strategy, you'll want to start by defining your goals.

Write down the specific targets you want to achieve, such as:

• Clicks/traffic

• Engagement

• Reach/subscriber numbers

Use the SMART model to help you put together good objectives: specific, measurable, attainable, relevant, and time-bound. This will help make sure that your objectives are specific, have a deadline, and are do-able.

Of course, you also need to be able to measure your progress accurately. At this stage of strategizing, establish what your KPIs (key performance indicators) are to help you measure your results.

Commit to a schedule

Consistency is very important on YouTube if you want to keep growing your channel. As with blogging, the more content you put out there, the better the chances you'll reach a wider audience.

Most successful YouTubers have a very strict publishing schedule – and they stick to it. These YouTubers also promote new videos to their audience on other social media platforms so that even those who haven't subscribed to their channel can still know when a new video is coming out. While you're setting up a YouTube marketing strategy for your business, consider how often you can realistically commit to posting new content and make sure you can stick to it.

Once you determine how often you can post, you should also consider when you release your videos. According to Oberlo, most viewers watch YouTube videos in the evenings and on weekends. The best time to post your content is early afternoons during the week or early Saturday and Sunday mornings so that your videos will be indexed by the time your potential viewers are searching.

Plus, at this stage, make a note of all the holidays and events coming up that are relevant to your audience so you'll know in advance about any opportunities to create any special content.

Types of marketing videos

So, now that you know what your goals are and when you want to publish, the question is, what types of videos can you create?

It's important to keep things varied in order to keep your audience entertained and coming back for more. Plus, it's worth experimenting early with different types of videos so you can understand which ones work best and which ones don't.

Here are a few ideas to get you started:

• **Listicles:** Listicles are a very popular content format, both as blog posts and as media (videos, images, infographics, etc.). You can create listicles that highlight your products or services – like "The 10 most innovative ways you can use (your product)" – or they can be educational, informational, or entertaining. Just remember, the lists should always be relevant to your audiences' interests and your business niche.

• **How-to videos:** How-to videos tend to perform very well because they provide a lot of value to the viewer. For example, if you were selling social media software, you could create how-to videos showing your viewers how to get started with

Twitter marketing or how to grow your Facebook following. You can look to top performing blog posts for material for these videos, or you can develop a plan for a recurring series. JetBlue has a series of "Flight Etiquette" videos that emphasize how not to travel:

• **Behind-the-scenes videos:** YouTube is a social network – the keyword here being "social." One of the ways to humanize your brand and show that you're more than just a product or service is to share some behind-the-scenes videos. For example, Sprout Social has an entire collection of videos with members of their team:

• **Product videos:** Video is a great way to showcase your own products or services. These product videos could walk viewers how to use certain features, highlighting new product updates, or announce new offerings for your business. MailChimp often publishes videos talking about their products:

• **Case studies:** Another way you can promote

your business and your products or services is to create video case studies of your clients. These case studies don't need to deal exclusively with your product: they can focus on client origin stories, recent achievements, or plans for the future. Hootsuitepublishes videos of their work with different brands:

• **Interviews:** Interviewing well-known experts and influencers from your niche is another good way to attract new viewers. These experts will have their own following, so if they're promoting the video as well, they can help drive traffic to your YouTube channel.

Managing your YouTube channel

Now that you have a YouTube marketing strategy and some video ideas to get started, you want to focus on managing your channel. Engagement is a big part of YouTube, so it's extremely important to take the time to not only respond to any comments you get, but also to drive engagement in other ways.

A good way to manage your account is to use a tool to help automate the process. Agorapulse lets you pre-moderate your comments, check and respond to comments from your dashboard's social inbox (which you can do as part of a team + you can assign tasks), as well as monitor YouTube for mentions of your brand in videos and comments. Other useful management features include saved replies (to respond to comments with a few clicks) and a social CRM tool to help keep track of your subscribers and connections.

Another good option for channel management is VidIQ, which you can use to keep track of comments and respond when necessary, to collaborate with your team members, and to discover useful keywords and tags for optimizing your videos.

Here are a few more YouTube tips to boost your engagement and views:

• Check your comments every day so you can respond promptly

• Use monitoring to find other mentions of your brand and identify engagement opportunities

• Ask questions of your viewers in your videos, as well as in your video descriptions to encourage them to leave a comment

• Use the "Community" tab (located in your channel's main page) to post images, GIFs, and video previews, as well as to poll your subscribers. For example, Evan Carmichael regularly posts polls asking his subscribers what they want to see in his upcoming videos:

Youtube Video SEO: What You Need To Know

As I mentioned earlier, YouTube is one of the top search engines in the world, which is one of the reasons why it's such an attractive promotional tool for businesses. Just imagine all the potential reach with almost two billion monthly users!

What this means is, quite simply, that if you take the time to optimize your videos and you produce quality video content on a regular basis, you can dramatically increase your chances of reaching a wide and targeted audience.

So, how exactly do you optimize your YouTube videos?

There are several important factors that count towards your search results ranking; some are completely in your control – like the keywords you use and how you use them – while with others, you don't have as much power over them (like how many people subscribe immediately after viewing one of your videos).

Here are some of the most important video ranking factors that you need to know about:

• **Your channel's keywords:** Use the right tags to make sure that YouTube knows what your channel is about.

• **Video headlines and descriptions:** Research keywords to find out what your audience is looking for and use these keywords in your video headlines and your descriptions. (Quick tip: the closer the keyword is to the beginning of the headline, the better!)

• **Video tags:** In addition to keywords, you need to add tags to your videos – research tags to find out which ones perform best.

• **Video transcript:** Including a video transcript is a great way to make your video more scrapable by search bots. It's also good for viewers: if they need to check spelling of a word or can't increase the volume to hear the video, they can still access the content.

• **Watch time:** Your total video watch time (how many minutes/hours/etc. people watched of your videos) also counts towards your ranking. The bigger the watch time, the better!

• **Thumbnail Image:** The thumbnail image will be visible whenever your video is indexed, so this should be compelling and relevant.

• **Engagement:** YouTube also looks at your channel's engagement, including how many likes/dislikes you get, as well as how many comments and shares.

• **Subscriber numbers:** This doesn't just mean how many YouTube subscribers you have. As I mentioned earlier, how many people subscribe after viewing one of your videos also matters. These subscribers show that your video was relevant and provided value to the viewer.

In terms of useful SEO tools, TubeBuddy is one of the best options because it has so many video SEO features, including:

• YouTube keyword research tools to help you find the right long-tail keywords to target

• Tag explorer, for discovering popular tags for your channel and your videos

• Keyword rank tracking to easily track your videos' ranking and success

• A/B testing for videos

• View and copy video tags

This last feature that allows you to check videos and see what tags they used. This is very useful as you can check very popular videos that rank highly (and are relevant to your own niche/videos) and see which tags helped them get to this stage.

When you're using your YouTube content on your other channels or on your website, make sure the video is the feature of the page for the best chance of ranking. Search crawlers won't go searching for a video hidden low on a page, and Google will typically only index the first video.

Optimizing your video content is important for establishing your YouTube marketing strategy, and it can also help with content while you're getting started. Keyword research is a great tool for finding video ideas. Before you create any new videos, take the time to research keywords and create videos based on the keywords you want to target.

Next step: YouTube marketing success

If it's used right, YouTube can be a great way to promote brand awareness and reach more potential customers. You can make sure your YouTube marketing strategy is bound for success by getting started with these key steps:

• Strategize your YouTube presence ahead of time and plan your videos in advance to make sure you publish new content regularly

• Create different types of videos to appeal to a wider audience

• Take the time to engage with your subscribers and viewers, as well as try to boost engagement with every video

• Optimize your channel and your videos for the

YouTube search engine to boost your reach

CHAPTER 5

TACTICS FOR AN EFFECTIVE YOUTUBE MARKETING STRATEGY

When it comes to content marketing, video is an up-and-comer, and it's making a stir. According to the State of Inbound 2017 Report, video content is cited to be the top disruptor in the marketing world. More than ever, consumers want to learn and connect with brands through video content, and brands are listening.

The results of video marketing are undeniable—

52% of marketing professionals worldwide list video as the type of content with the best ROI. For many businesses, the easiest part about making a video is deciding where to post it. As the most popular video hosting website by far, choosing to upload your video to YouTube is an obvious choice.

However, even with all of the awesome benefits of video marketing, only 9% of small businesses are on YouTube. Why? It's the second largest search engine behind Google and is used by 1.3 billion people worldwide. The number one reason business owners give for not having a YouTube content strategy is that they simply don't have enough understanding of how to produce video content.

Here, we outline 6 tactics for an effective YouTube marketing strategy:

1. Do Your Research

This is, of course, the first step to any content marketing strategy. Just like you wouldn't write a blog before knowing what your audience wants to read about or how blog writing works, diving headfirst into video content without any information isn't the smartest idea.

The best thing to do when developing your YouTube marketing strategy is to see what your competitors are doing. What kind of video content are they producing? How successful is their video content? Are there gaps in the content they produce? Look at what is already out there and what is or is not succeeding before you begin to build out your own content.

2. Create Useful, Creative Content

When creating content for YouTube, it's important to consider why people are interacting with video content more than any other content type. It's because they find video to be more personal and engaging than blogs, whitepapers and ebooks, and are looking for the entertainment value of video paired with the utility of conventional formats.

So what does this mean for video creators? The

number one thing to keep in mind is that you must keep your content interesting. While people would prefer to watch a video tutorial, if you create an unappealing video of someone droning on about how to use a product, the customer will likely abandon the video, and in some cases, the product.

You have an endless variety of video topics to choose from. You could create content on how to use a product, success stories of people who've used it, office culture videos, demo videos—if it can be presented in a creative, useful way, it's worth exploring.

3. Partner With Others

YouTube is dominated by a unique form of celebrity that has only been around for the past few years—the YouTuber. These stars build huge followings around their channels, which can garner millions of followers and billions of views.

While there's a common misconception that YouTubers attract only the millennial audience, thousands of popular content creators geared towards older individuals would disagree. There are YouTube stars for every interest—while the stereotypical YouTuber vlogs about beauty, video gaming or fashion, many of them make videos about home organization, parenting, car repair and everything else that could interest a consumer.

Try and reach out to a YouTuber that makes videos about your industry, or one who resonates with your desired customer. This is an extremely effective way to bring attention to your brand and content, and is a win-win for both parties involved. When you collaborate with someone who has a similar audience to yours, the cross-exposure is both organic and lucrative.

4. Link Back To Your Website

While this may sound simplistic, it's actually one of the best ways to drive traffic to your website. This can be done in two ways—you can add an annotation within your video that will take users to your site once they click on it, or you could add a link in your description box below the video.

5. Create Calls-to-Action

While inserting traditional button CTAs isn't an option in YouTube marketing, you still need to create calls-to-action for your users. What are you asking them to do at the end of each video?

Well, the answer should depend on which stage of the funnel the video is geared towards. If it's an introductory video, ask them to like and subscribe to your page for more content. If it's a demo video, ask them to check out your website for more information. Creating calls-to-action in your videos will actively guide your viewers through the sales funnel and help you see results faster.

6. Be Consistent

It's understandable that many businesses find a YouTube channel harder to maintain than, say, a blog—YouTube videos can rack up production costs quickly, and the script-writing, filming and editing can take a lot of time. However, YouTube must be treated the same as any other part of your content strategy.

Which is to say, if you aren't consistent, you're not going to see any results.

YouTube marketing is like all other marketing, and if you're going to do it, you have to be all in. Make an introductory video on your channel so that subscribers know how often you're going to post—and once you've gotten into a rhythm, stick with it.

However, consistency doesn't end with how often you post videos—you also have to be consistent with their quality. If you start off posting well-produced, thoughtful videos, and soon begin to post poorly filmed and written content, you're going to see a drop in your following. When you post your first video, make sure subsequent videos maintain, if not improve, the initial quality. In order to build a following and see results, you absolutely must be consistent.

Creating video content can be a time-consuming and lengthy process, but is incredibly important in the visual age. No matter your audience, consumers of all stripes are choosing video over other content types, so it's more critical than ever to make sure your YouTube marketing strategy is keeping up.

.

CHAPTER 6

YOUTUBE MARKETING STRATEGIES

YouTube has emerged as the most popular video sharing website allowing businesses, digital marketers and professionals to exhibit their videos on the platform. Posting explainer videos on YouTube can bestow a brand identity to your business within a short span of time while giving the viewers a better understanding of the product line. Apart from giving the ideal exposure to the video marketing for your brand, YouTube is also a great place to post videos and earn money online.

The explainer video about your product, brand or business plays a crucial role in educating the target audience in a interesting way. Ideally, a video of 3 minutes duration can give the viewers much better understanding about the product than a long text that is often boring for many to read. If you are good at creating engaging videos at periodical intervals, consider placing them on your YouTube channel to make money online.

The foremost problem that the clients often encounter on the platform is the difficulty to get visitors to see their videos. There is already tremendous competition from niche videos on the website. This is not a problem if you have a plan to promote the videos. To help you to get free views on YouTube, we have provide the most effective strategies used by experienced digital marketers to drive views, subscribers and likes to their videos. You do not have to be a marketing expert to do this, just follow these tips to see the difference.

1. Use the Facebook Native Video Uploader

One of the traditional ways most people assort to promote videos on social media is to share the link on Facebook and similar other sites. In a recent research, it is revealed that the shared links get fewer views than any video uploaded on Facebook.

Use the Facebook's Native Video Uploader tool to upload the YouTube videos. For successful audience engagement to your YouTube channel, add a call to action with the video on Facebook inviting them to subscribe to your videos on YouTube. Do not forget to add the link to your YouTube channel with the shared post and the call to action.

2. Maintain a Regular Schedule for Uploading Videos

The niche audiences take interest in channels where they find new videos periodically. If you do not post new videos on the channel, the traffic rate and views will fall in due course. Try to maintain regularity when uploading new videos. Choose a certain day of the week and keep the schedule same for every week. The subscribers are notified automatically when you post new videos on the channel. If the audiences receive the notification at proper instances, you will get views regularly at the channel.

3. Embed the YouTube Video URLs on Your Blog or Website

This is one of the best ways to get free YouTube views. If you have a high traffic blog or website, embedding the videos on the blog can help in increasing the views significantly.

When doing so, place the YouTube videos URL amid relevant text contents with some images to make the entire combination look like a high quality blog post.

If you want to embed videos on a blog or website, make sure that the niche of your blog and the videos are the same. This will attract niche audiences not only subscribe to the YouTube channel but also engage them to achieve improved results with the blog traffic.

Do share the blog post and the videos across all social media platforms to get greater exposure.

4. Add a Proper Title to Every Single Video on Your YouTube Channel

The title is the first and prime factor your

audiences will take note of before watching the video. The title should be very precise and give clear idea of the content to expect in the video. For best results with the SEO, it is mandatory to keep the title within 50 characters. Long titles are cut off from the view of the audiences lowering the chances of getting views. For greater impact, try to include the main keyword in the title.

5. Write a Small Catchy Description for Every Video

The small description at the bottom of the video can convey valuable information to the viewers about the video content. Worthy short descriptions can help to get YouTube views for free in greater numbers. While writing your description, take note of the following factors:

• Write the description in easy words keeping it short and to the point

• The description must match exactly the contents in the video

• Use relevant keywords to make sure the target audience can find it easily

• Add a description for every single video and make sure to write separate one for each

Using the keywords in the description is very important to tell the audience about the topic in the video. You need to dedicate some time into the research process to find the best suitable keywords to rank up high in the SERPs (search engine result pages). Use the top keyword research tools like the Adwords Keyword Planner or Google Trends.

You can add links to your website or blog in the description. Putting a link to the playlist will also help the audience to navigate to other videos on your channel. If they find the videos interesting, there are greater chances of building a strong subscribers' list.

6. Use Long Tail Keywords to Bestow Better

Experience with the Search Results

Not all audiences looking for similar content on YouTube or search engines enter the same keyword. You must try many alternatives to build up a larger audience base. Use semantic keywords and long tail keywords to optimize your video content.

Try to find the long keyword phrases you think the audiences may possibly use to find similar contents. Ubersuggest is a wonderful keyword tool to find long-tail keywords. You can use the most powerful in the list to place in the title or the video description.

This is the best among many tried and tested video marketing strategies. This will take some time especially if you are not well acquainted with digital marketing techniques.

7. Take Care to Maintain Short Video Duration

Buffer Social recently published an analytical report based on their research on video length that grabs the audiences' attention. Based on the studies it has been found that the ideal length of a YouTube explainer video should be 2 minutes 54 seconds. On an average, your video should not be more than 3 minutes and less than 2 minutes to get the desired outcome.

8. Be Very Specific with Your Keywords

If you want to succeed in promoting the videos on YouTube, the ultimate aim should be to achieve better results with organic or unpaid searches. In other words, you need to get free YouTube views as much as possible. Search engine optimization is your ultimate goal to provide better experience to the viewers hitting the play button to watch the video.

You can also use the autocomplete feature on YouTube to find the best suitable keyword alternatives to use to promote the channel. This is very easy to do. Start typing your video topic on the YouTube search bar. You will see similar other terms appearing as suggestions on the screen. If any of the options match your video content, consider the phrases and work on them for search engine optimization.

Once you have chosen a set of keywords, perform a Google search to see the competitors' videos in the list. The presence of similar videos in the list shows that there is a great audience base looking for these videos.

9. Arrange Your Videos in Playlists on Customized Thumbnails

If you are posting a series of educational videos, you need to create different playlists for a particular group of videos. Use proper keywords for the playlists to attract more visitors. You can create customized video thumbnails where the series of similar videos will appear. The audiences will easily find the section of videos they want to see on the channel.

Use relevant captivating snapshots and annotations on the thumbnails to raise the interest in the visitors at the channel.

10. Add a Dynamic Intro in the Video

It is important for the audience to understand what they are going to see in the video. Many people miss the description written below. Your video must start with an intro. The intro should explain the topic properly.

The duration of the intro plays a crucial role in retaining the audiences. Your intro should not be longer than 10 seconds. Ideally, the video marketers try to keep a 5 seconds short intro. If your intro is too long, the audiences may leave and click on any other similar one in the list.

11. Add a Call to Action at the End of the Video

The ultimate way to get free views on YouTube regularly is to have a large subscribers' list. You can add a call to action immediately at the end of the video content asking the viewers subscribe to your channel. If they really like the video, there are greater chances to get a positive result.

Some people place the call to action in the intro. This may make the intro duration longer. Unless the visitor watches the entire content, he is unsure whether it is good to subscribe to the entire list. Try experimenting with the placement to see the difference. You can edit the videos accordingly later.

12. Add a Catchy Trailer on the Homepage of Your YouTube Channel

Many viewers visit the channel homepage to get more information apart from the watched video before subscribing. Add an informative and engaging trailer on the homepage. This trailer appears on the top of the channel page. This is an interesting YouTube feature. The trailer plays automatically only for the non-subscribers visiting the channel for the first time. The regular subscribers will not be bored with such repetitive content.

13. Use the 'Subscribe' Button in Solid Color at Appropriate Places

There is a red Subscribe button at the bottom of all videos on YouTube. You can get greater results by adding a similar button on your blog or website. Add unique call to action with the button to prompt the website audience to subscribe to the channel. The position of the Subscribe button should be adjacent to the embedded video on the blog or website.

14. Add a Button and Call to Action for Inviting the Visitors to Like the Video

While a large subscribers' list ensures you will get regular views on the YouTube channel, the greater number of likes on the video is another useful element to grow the audience. When a viewer sees a considerable number of likes on a video, he or she is sure of the quality of the content. If your videos get more likes, it is favorable for growing an ever-increasing audience base.

There is a 'Like' button below all videos on YouTube. You can add a similar solid color button on your blog and website placed next to the embedded YouTube video. This is not only a great factor to get free YouTube views, drive audiences to the channel but also grow the blog traffic. The videos with greater number of likes get the chance to range higher on the YouTube and Google platforms. Higher your video position, the greater is the number of views you can expect.

15. Incorporate the YouTube Widget on Your Blog and Website

This is very easy and catches the attention of the audiences on the blog or website. The widget looks like a small but notable tool displaying all your videos. You can add the YouTube widget to a blog by pasting the provided code.

16. Give Replies to the Comments

The audiences leave comments below your videos sharing their experience, opinion and sometimes queries. At times, you may get negative comments too. Reply to all the comments politely. If there is a query, try to give the best possible answer or solution. Your nice gesture is pleasing to the audiences. Sometimes, people view these comments first before seeing the video. If they find you responsive to the comments, they may take greater interest in subscribing to the channel.

The comments are like feedback allowing you to improve the videos in future. It will help you with the work for the upcoming projects, video marketing strategies etc.

17. Build a Community Relation with Other YouTube Channels

Co-branding is an advanced online marketing strategy and implies to promote your YouTube channel too. You can work with other YouTube channel admins to promote each other's videos. You need to get along this job through proper marketing channels. The video marketer handling a lot of projects apply such simple techniques to grow target audience base.

18. Use the GrowViews Tool

If you are looking for co-branding without spending much time in contacting other YouTubers, building relationships and others, the GrowViews is the best tool to consider to get free views on YouTube.

The tool is designed specifically for directing organic traffic to YouTube. With this tool, you will get more people to watch your videos, subscribers returning regularly to watch your new videos, likes etc. You can get started with a free plan and stay on it for unlimited period getting views in exchange when you view videos from other subscribers.

The GrowViews tool is a time saver option for internet marketers, business owners, YouTube channel admins and all others. You do not have to waste time and energy contacting other YouTubers and convincing them to promote your videos. GrowViews has a massive clientele base with a network of more than 111685 channels.

There is much to explore at GrowViews. The company also offers special cost-effective packages for internet marketing agencies to help them accomplish the video marketing projects effectively. The company has strict anti-spamming policies and does not use auto bots or other unfair means to drive traffic.

For more information on the tool and its functionalities, visit www.growviews.com.

19. Ask Your Loyal Audience to Share the Videos

Study the analytics report at your YouTube account dashboard to find the most promising audiences on your channel. You may contact them to share the videos with their friends.

You can also place a generic call to action below the video with a 'Share' button asking everyone to share the video with his or her friends and others.

20. Use Your Email Subscribers List to Promote

the Videos

If you already have a powerful email list of interested subscribers' base on your blog or website, it is good to utilize the same list to promote your videos too. You can send a small newsletter to the listed email addresses with a personal note encouraging them to watch the embedded video on the blog or website at first.

The strategy is beneficial in two ways:

• You will get more views to the blog or website

• There is a greater chance of getting a subscribers' base on the YouTube channel

This strategy works splendid if you are already running an education or tutorial website. If your videos are also related to the educational material in a series, there is very high chance to get YouTube views for free, build a larger audience base and subscribers on the YouTube channel.

Note: When sending video links the email subscribers, make sure it is of use and interest to the recipient. If the video content does not match your blog content where the person has subscribed, it can result in loss of blog traffic.

21. Consider Video Optimization across Search Engines and All Social Media Platforms

Nowadays, Google and all other standard search engines place the videos in search results for all keywords. Consider optimizing the videos for the keywords for search engines to get free YouTube views.

Upload videos on all social media websites- Twitter, Tumblr, Google+, Facebook, Pinterest, Instagram, LinkedIn etc. You can also consider SlideShare to share your videos too.

22. Synchronize Your Google+ Account with the YouTube Channel

If you have a huge community at Google+ with whom you chat regularly about similar topics, it is beneficial to utilize this list to grow traffic on the YouTube channel. Use the 'Hangouts On Air' feature to record and upload the Hangouts automatically to YouTube. You will then be able to promote your channel on Google+, the most densely crowded social media platform next to Facebook. # Bonus Tip: Promote Your YouTube Channel It takes great effort to promote individual videos to get subscribers to the YouTube. Consider promoting your channel as well. You can place the trailer video on the channel across social media platforms to get more visitors. All the above-mentioned strategies also apply when trying to promote your channel.

The Bottom Line- Keep Tracking the Analytics and Experimenting with New Methods

While the first step to grow income on this video sharing site is to get YouTube views for free as much as possible, it is essential to consider some important facts.

• It takes time to grow audience on any YouTube channel

• Researching with the keywords is a time consuming process and you will need to dedicate some effort for at least a couple of months or more to get the desired results

• Building your audience base in a continuous process wherein you can keep experimenting with new ideas to bring in a change

• The ultimate goal to achieve long-term success with your YouTube channel is to optimize your contents for unpaid searches

If you want to outreach the neck tight competition and grow the brand identity for a new or existing business, the video marketing can make all the difference. The market experts opine that this form of promotional strategy strengthens the content marketing project making it convenient for the brand owners to get quick results in terms of conversions.

Not all videos are same nor are the audiences. Therefore, it is impossible to predict a specific formula for sure success. Keep trying out different methods while tracking the changes. This will give you the idea on what works best for the niche videos on your YouTube channel.

YOUTUBE STRATEGIES FOR SMALL BUSINESSES

Did you know that your audience loves visual content the most? Amongst visual content, videos are a favourite of the audience. Whether you own a retail business or offer B2B services, there's enormous scope with videos, to create content that would engage your audience. A lot can be done to market your brand on this video sharing platform.

If you don't have a YouTube channel for your brand, you need to get one now. The best part about YouTube is that you can use your brand channel to log into multiple google accounts simultaneously. So, a YouTube channel will allow for streamlined workflow in teams.

Also, YouTube has a huge viewership. Leverage it

the right way to reach out to big audience segments. Set up a strong YouTube marketing strategy that helps you win over your audience.

As we approach new year, new trends, features and updates on the platform as well as in the social media marketing industry will affect your strategy. A good YouTube marketing strategy accounts for leveraging the new as well as the old.

If you want to grow your business now and forever, follow these startegies to master the YouTube marketing for year and years to come:

1. Build your YouTube brand channel

Your YouTube channel should spin out your brand's story to the people. From your channel icon to channel description, everything should speak your brand's voice. Add your brand's logo to the YouTube channel icon. Add a custom YouTube banner as well, with social media icons leading your audience to your social media handles across platforms.

In the 'About' section of your YouTube channel, add a brief description of your brand. Your description should introduce every new visitor to your brand and reflect your brand voice. Put calls to action leading to your website or any other pages you want to lead your audience to.

Finally, divide your videos into different playlists. You can create branded playlists with names unique to your brand. Categorise playlists into webinars, behind the scenes etc., depending upon your video content.

2. Consistently create and add compelling videos to your channel

Create video content that gets your audience talking. Most importantly, use YouTube videos to bring out your brand's story.

Are you a B2B brand? You can create YouTube videos that complement your blog or website content. Bring your customers to give quick reviews of your brand. Ask them to share the experience of using your products, working with your brand and so on to take your YouTube marketing plan to the next level. Create and run a separate Video blog channel for your brand and interact with your audience using the platform regularly.

Interview industry professionals, seniors and subject matter experts. Informative video content is most popular with the audiences. Post step by step videos and tutorials on how to use your products or services.

At the same time, keep posting videos consistently on your channel. Find out the right time to post content, when the audience is most active on the platform. Add videos to your channel accordingly.

3. Leverage YouTube tools and features

YouTube has a host of tools and features that can help you enhance your YouTube marketing strategy 2019. Use end screens and cards to add your desired calls to action. Shared a video on how to assemble a product? Lead your audience to other videos on how to use the product and other similar content from your playlists.

Add transcripts your videos. Make your video content universal by adding closed captions. It cuts out the language barrier and makes your content consumable by audiences across borders. At the same time, you can reach out to the disabled with this YouTube video feature. A keyword-optimized video transcript helps enhance your YouTube SEO as well.

These incredible tools come as a part of your YouTube channel. Make the most of these, to level up on your YouTube Marketing strategy.

4. Optimise your YouTube video description and thumbnails

Since your YouTube video thumbnails and description are the ones that provide a glimpse into your content, optimize these for better results. Your YouTube thumbnail should push YouTube users to click and watch your video. The most important elements of a good YouTube thumbnail image include a picture and a caption. Add a popping image and caption that draws the attention of your audience. Use facial-closeups for best response. The idea is to create a visual representation of the video content in the thumbnail.

Equally important in your YouTube marketing strategy 2019 is your video description. Make all your YouTube video descriptions keyword optimized to enhance YouTube SEO. Also, make sure that your YouTube video descriptions align and complement your YouTube video content. Apart from using keywords, use catchy phrases that push the users to hit the play button on your videos.

5. Add YouTube stories to your YouTube Marketing Strategy

After Instagram and Facebook, YouTube hops on to the stories' bandwagon. YouTube now has the stories feature which allows for you to add short, mobile-only videos that expire after 7 days. YouTube offers this feature to creators with more than 10,000 subscribers on the platform. Easily create YouTube stories in a matter of seconds with the tap button on your profile and then edit them. Trim your YouTube stories and add filters, music, text, stickers, and even links to your videos.

As a creator, this tool allows you to diversify on your content on the platform. With this new feature and the tools that come along with it, you can build a strong relationship with your community. It will also help you boost engagement.

Create compelling stories that generate interactions with viewers. Respond to all the comments and expand your community.

6. Optimise Video Titles For YouTube Voice Search

Enhance your YouTube SEO by optimising title for YouTube voice search. People use YouTube voice search to find videos quickly, without having to use their fingers to type out the video titles.

Since voice search is an easier, hassle free way to get YouTube video results, you need to ensure your videos appear before your audience.

Most importantly, optimise your YouTube video title to make it SEO friendly. Imagine yourself using YouTube voice search for your videos. Would you go for a longer YouTube video title or a shorter one? Most people will use a small number of keywords to describe their YouTube query.

The language will be less formal and more conversational.

So, frame a YouTube title that includes important keywords, is short and simple and has a conversational tone. This will improve your YouTube SEO to a great extent and eventually increase your views on the platform.

7. Influencer Marketing On YouTube

Include Influencer marketing as a part of your YouTube marketing strategy 2019. There are 3 main benefits of partnering with an Influencer:

1. Access to a larger audience

2. Access to another creator's skills

3. Diversification of your content

And all these benefits add up to bring more engagement for your brand. Find out niche Influencer. Someone whose niche aligns with your brand. Using Unbox Social's social media analytics tool, track different Influencers from your niche. The Industry feed feature on the tool dashboard allows you to track as many Influencers as you want and get regular updates about them.

Monitor their activity and zero down on one Influencer. Approach them and bring them on board. You can use Influencers to churn out great quality video content. Leverage their content creation skills and influence to your best.

Ask them to do product reviews, feature on your channel for account takeovers, or make them your brand ambassadors. There are many ways in which you can use Influencer marketing as a part of your

YouTube marketing strategy.

At the same time keep track of all the trends and watch out for outdated Influencer marketing practices that you may be indulging in.

8. Use YouTube Ads

Paid content will continue to be an integral part of a good YouTube strategy 2019. A sureshot way to make your videos appear before your audience is through the advertising option.

YouTube Ads come in 6 different formats-skippable TrueView in-stream Ads, 6-second bumper Ads, sponsored cards, overlay Ads, display Ads and Trueview Discovery Ads which appear on the homepage, alongside search results and next to related videos.

If you aren't using YouTube Ads to market your brand, do it now and check out the results for yourself.

9. Monitor your Competitors

Monitoring your competitors is an integral part of every business and marketing strategy. Competitor analysis can easily be done by visiting their YouTube channel itself. Identify their videos with most views to identify content that most people resonate with. Use such content to draw inspiration for future video posts.

Skim through their comments to find out any mentions of your brand. In case you spot your brand mentions, make sure to respond to each of the comments.

Also find out if any of their Ads are featuring on your videos. If that is the case, you can block these on the Google Ads manager.

10. Track and report on important metrics to learn from them

An important part of YouTube marketing strategy 2019 is to track your performance and watch out for important metrics. Use a social media analytics and reporting tool such as Unbox Social.

With this tool, you can track all relevant social media metrics and then generate customized reports of the same.

Use Unbox Social to monitor metrics such as watch time retention, top videos, video-wise engagement. Monitor your audience metrics along age, gender and location. Target audience segments accordingly.

Also generate reports to uncover all your social media metrics for the desired time period. In a matter of 4 steps, you can pull out a YouTube analytics report with Unbox Social. You can set scheduled reports for time periods that you will set.

Use these reports to identify content with better engagement and response from your audience. Take inspiration from such content to inform your content strategies.

11. Keep up with industry trends and updates

To be on top of your game in any industry, it is important to keep track of industry trends and updates. The social media industry is a dynamic one in itself. New features and trends in the industry as well as on the platform will inform your YouTube marketing plan.

Use Unbox Social's personalized feeds to derive information and daily updates on your industry from your chosen sources.

Get an edge over the others by always staying on top of news, trends and updates in your industry.

Conclusively, a good YouTube marketing strategy involves leveraging all the tools and features at your disposal and employing them to build engagement. It also involves keeping a watch on the industry as well as your competitors.

Here's a snapshot of pointers summing up on important tips for YouTube marketing strategy for your business:

- Build and enhance your YouTube channel, to reflect your brand voice

- Add compelling videos that add value to the

audience and make sure to post consistently

-       Leverage YouTube tools such as transcripts, end screens and cards and annotations

-       Add an eye catching thumbnail image and optimise video descriptions for SEO

-       Include YouTube stories as a part of your YouTube marketing strategy 2019 to build on your community and diversify your content

-       Optimise YouTube video titles for YouTube voice search- Use simpler, shorter titles

-    Use Influencer marketing for access to a larger audience, leverage another creator's skills and create versatile content

-       Continue using YouTube Ads for a sure shot appearance before your target audience

-    Keep track of your competitors

-    Uncover insights about important video metrics using social media analytics' tools

- Stay on top of major industry trends and news

CONCLUSION

Whether you decide to use video, audio, or both to increase your site's exposure, this YouTube marketing strategy is a great source to consider for promoting your company.

By creating and uploading a video that represents what you stand for, it allows the Internet masses to get a first hand glimpse at what you and your business are about. You may have already created articles, tags, and email dumping as some of the strategies you already have in place. The ideal thing about using YouTube is that you can combine the sources you already have in place with the video/audio channel you created on YouTube. The glory of this entire idea is that it is free of cost to do. Yes, it does take some time to do it correctly and maintain it's effectiveness, but you will not pay a cent to post it for folks to view.

This YouTube marketing strategy is becoming more and more popular by the day. Many businesses prefer not to use YouTube as a source of marketing their services or products, but YouTube is one of the top rated visited sites on the entire Internet at this time. It's popularity grows on a daily basis and thus gives many business owners the exposure of their business they so drastically need and desire. It is a superior traffic generator for websites, and if the video is done well, in a unique interesting fashion, then the hits you receive on your site will increase in no time.

However, YouTube alone can greatly influence the success of your social media marketing campaign; however it also works well with Facebook and Twitter. With the many great tools offered, if you aren't using YouTube as part of your marketing, you are missing out on an incredible way to attract new customers.